Staying Put

One Englishman's Fight to Remain in Spain

J.J.Birtwell

Text copyright © 2015 J.J.Birtwell

All rights reserved. No part of this publication may be reproduced, stored in a retrieval system, or transmitted, in any form or by any means, without the prior permission in writing of the publisher.

1

When just a sliver of blue sky remained between the sun and the sparsely wooded hills to the west Jack always downed trowel, book or coffee cup and sat down in his chair on the porch to watch the sunset. He must have seen thousands of them from that very porch, he reflected, and after an especially hot August day today's sunset would be a welcome one.

When the last tinges of red had left the sky the consequences of that morning's calculations forced their way back into his mind. He closed his eyes and saw only dark clouds. Instead of his neat little house two miles from the village he saw a council flat in the worst part of Accrington, his native Lancashire town. His view of cultivated fields and distant cordilleras was replaced by that of a damp street and parked cars. His acre or so of land was reduced to a sodden, sun-starved window box. When he opened his eyes his thriving tomato plants came into focus. If his financial prospects were as bad as they seemed – and he knew that they were – a few summers from now he might be buying his fruit and veg at Asda.

The thought of cycling into the village the next morning cheered him momentarily. It was Saturday, market day, and after a little banter with the stallholders he would repair to the bar for breakfast, a glass or two of wine, and more friendly chatter. He enjoyed his thrice-weekly trips to the village, but what he liked most of all was being in the country, working on his allotment, reading, thinking, enjoying the sun.

He had thought towns, especially English towns, were a thing of the past for him, but on turning sixty the previous week he had forced himself to take stock of his situation. Having spent the last twenty-five years in Spain, his British pension would be a pitiful affair, and as he had worked only casually for the last few years he doubted that the Spanish state would be coughing up much either.

Still, he thought, if he could manage now, he would manage even better when they threw him a few crumbs in five years' time. This reminded him to call Brian, his friend and employer. He entered the square, three-bedroom bungalow, opened most of the windows to let in the cooling air, and returned to the porch with his mobile phone.

"Brian, it's Jack. What've you got for me next week?"

"Not a lot, pal. We'll finish tiling round that pool on Monday and after that I'm buggered if I know. Are you coming in tomorrow morning?"

"Yes, I'll cycle in at about nine."

"Let's meet at Pam's bar at half past."

"OK, see you then."

It was unusual of Brian to want to meet up at the weekend and in his current state of mind Jack couldn't help feeling that something was amiss. Meeting at Pam's bar too. Of the three bars in the village Brian knew that Jack frequented the English bar the least. It wasn't that he had gone native exactly, but his Spanish was fluent and he hadn't spent almost half his life here to listen to his countrymen chattering about pools, conservatories and how you couldn't trust Spanish workers. Jack trusted some of his Spanish friends – Vicente and Salvador especially – with his life and he had only ended up working for Brian because they got on well, he paid well, and he only needed him two or three days a week. Vicente, a local copper who worked in not too distant

Monóvar, had been right though – that his decision to work cash in hand would come back to haunt him one day.

Perhaps Brian wanted to meet at Pam's bar – home ground for him – because he had some bad news to impart. At sixty Jack was still as fit as a butcher's dog, as they used to say back in Accrington, but if he said he didn't feel his age he'd be lying. His knees had started to ache at times, although cycling everywhere seemed to alleviate them, and that curse of all builders – a bad back – seemed to be hitting him more frequently of late.

Not that Jack was a builder by trade. He had come to Spain when he was thirty-five to teach English in the city of Murcia and escape from his dull office job for a while. He was recently divorced and, not having kids, he saw no reason not to prolong his belated 'year out' and after almost ten years in Murcia – the years that might produce a bit of a pension for him – he had invested some inheritance money in the house that had sheltered him so well for the last fifteen years; sheltered him physically and also from people, whom he found increasingly irksome unless he knew and liked them.

He knew that the other British folk, and there were plenty of them around now, thought him something of an oddity – almost a hermit, in fact – but the villagers, though most of them wouldn't want it for themselves, respected his preference for solitude. When he arrived among them at a sprightly forty-five they assumed his new car and year-long sabbatical from paid work meant that he was well off and he sensed that some subtle, and not so subtle, matchmaking was afoot.

After a brief dalliance with Esme, the local chemist and a recent divorcee, had cooled and changed into a long-lasting friendship, the commencement of his labouring duties for the recently arrived Brian, a highly skilled builder and carpenter from Hexham, instantly made him much less of a catch.

When he began to eschew his car in favour of an old mountain bike the mothers of unmarried or divorced daughters began to turn their attention to more promising suitors. Esme married a teacher from Jumilla and Jack became increasingly at ease with his bachelor status.

* * *

The next morning he set off down the dusty track to the village at a quarter past nine, not wishing to reach Pam's bar before Brian did. The sun was already high enough to make itself felt and he rode slowly up the last half mile of road past the wine cooperative, a row of ugly new houses, and the small but well-tended park and play area. The population of the village had recently topped three thousand for the first time since the 1950s, due mainly, but not wholly, to the influx of foreign residents.

Jack guessed that there were around a hundred 'rich' foreigners living in, and especially around, the village, and each time a new couple or family arrived the local tradesmen rubbed their hands together – literally, for he had been with a couple of them when they had done it. The new arrivals' penchant for restoring old properties and building pools, patios and boundary walls kept many people busy and had an important knock on effect. As well as Pam's bar, which had been closed for many years until she bought, renovated and reopened it in 2010, a new restaurant had recently appeared, as well as a small supermarket and a hairdresser's. Carmen's tiny post office was no longer in danger of closing. Ramón's hardware store had branched out into building supplies and Reme's moribund tobacconist's had expanded into adjacent premises to make room for newspapers, magazines, sweets and an unpredictable display of home-made cakes. These latter items annoyed Marco the baker no end until he produced a trump card from his off-white sleeve; an estate agency to be run by his clever, English-speaking daughter Marta.

Even at half past nine on a Saturday Jack saw a couple of grey heads seated across from Marta as she beguiled them with glossy photos and her heavily accented sales patter. Jack nodded at Marta, tutted to himself, and leant his bike against the wall of Pam's bar right next door. He popped his head through the bead curtains and, seeing no sign of Brian, decided to walk down the street to buy a paper. Yes, it was amazing what a hundred or so settlers could do for a place. Most of the people he knew thought it was, on the whole, a good thing. The newcomers spent money, were generally quiet, and the increasing vibrancy of the village made the youngsters less likely to leave.

"Look at Juan Sempere's son, Juanito," Vicente had said to Jack one afternoon after dropping by on his way home from work. "He wouldn't have found work here in a million years, the lazy devil, and there he is helping Ramón to sell bricks and cement to the *guiris*."

Guiri is a slightly disrespectful term for foreigners and it's usage in the village had increased a hundredfold in the last decade.

"Do they call me *guiri*?" Jack asked his friend.

"Not that I know of, and I'd arrest anyone who did."

"This is not your patch."

"It doesn't matter," he said, smiling and patting his holster.

"Have you even used that thing?"

"Only on the firing range. I drew it once many years ago when a drunk pulled a knife on me outside a pub in Monóvar."

"Would you have shot him?"

"Yes, in the foot. It would have been interesting, but the paperwork would have been endless."

Vicente was a slightly younger and darker version of himself, physically at least. Both men were about five ten, wiry and fit for their age. Both had blue eyes and a full head of greying hair, Jack's a shade lighter, befitting his five years' seniority. Temperamentally they were poles apart. Vicente loved being around people and had never been able to tempt Jack to go along to try out his main hobby, Latin dancing. Jack preferred to see people one-to-one and Vicente understood this. Sometimes they didn't see each other for a while, but they were best friends in the sense that each sought out the other when they had a serious problem.

Jack wished he were meeting Vicente now rather than Brian, but it was Brian who greeted him when he returned to Pam's bar with a copy of *El País* under his arm.

"Hello, Jack. What are you having?"

"Just a coffee, please," he said, looking from Brian to Pam.

"Coming right up, stranger," said the matronly lady from Shropshire. Jack liked her and used to call in more often, until the bead curtain had obscured the view inside from the street. Her tendency to introduce him to all her new customers had made his visits less frequent as small talk was not one of his strong points. As he carried his coffee to the table he reflected that if he were eventually forced to return to Accrington, he hoped that there would be someone as nice as her behind at least one of the café counters there.

"You look thoughtful," said Brian as Jack took the chair opposite him.

"You look tired," Jack said, noticing his friend's puffy eyes.

"Late night last night. We invited that new couple from Yorkshire round to dinner. He brought a bottle of whisky and wasn't planning on leaving any."

"Wrong side of the Pennines, mate," Jack said, purely out of habit. "Will they be putting any work your way?"

"That's what I'd hoped, of course, but it seems he's a handy bloke, so they might not. I'm just going outside for a quick smoke."

Before you tell me the bad news, Jack thought, as Brian's bulky form disappeared through the curtain. Brian was about fifty and had been one of the earliest English settlers in the village, just a year after himself. Back then he had been delighted to have someone from the same sort of background to speak English to and they had hit it off right away. Brian soon got a big restoration job and asked Jack to help him out. At first it was just mixing and carrying, but Brian had taught him a lot over the years and after his belated apprenticeship he now felt that he was a semi-skilled man at the very least. Shame that his back was no longer up to much.

"Yes, I was counting on them having at least a few little jobs for us," Brian said as he resumed his seat. He pushed his hand back over his bristly grey hair before tapping his thick fingers on the table and looking at his coffee.

"If you've got some bad news, Brian, just spit it out. We are friends, after all."

"Right, well... the thing is, with the way things are I don't think I'm going to need you much from now on, unless... until things pick up."

"I see," Jack said, reassuring his friend with a smile.

"After we finish that tiling on Monday I've only got a few small jobs lined up. With the expense of being self-employed here, I really need to do those jobs on my own, to make them last till something bigger comes up."

"I understand. Don't worry, I can get along for a while without working. You know I don't spend much. A big job will come along soon, one always does."

"I hope so," said Brian, a shadow of what Jack thought might be guilt passing over his face. He coughed and sipped his coffee. "The trouble is that the local builders have started to get their acts together now, especially Martínez, who sent his lad away to Alicante to learn English. He's back now and has been doing the rounds with some new cards they've had printed in English and Spanish."

"He's a lousy builder," said Jack.

"Yes, lousy and cheap. The Brits that are coming out now don't have as much money as they used to. They snap up a cheap house, but then haven't much left to do it up with."

"Most of them won't last. Especially the younger ones."

"No, but whether they last or not, they're no use to us."

"Listen, Brian. You finish that tiling yourself. It might give you another day's work. Don't worry about me. I'm more concerned about my long-term prospects than a few euros here or there."

"How's that?"

Jack shared the results of the previous morning's calculations with Brian.

"Bloody hell, that doesn't sound good. You want to get online and check up on how much you'll have coming to you from your British pension."

"Online? You mean the computer? You know I don't see eye to eye with those things."

"No, me neither, but Liz is well clued up now since we got internet at the house. I can ask her to look into it for you."

"Thanks, Brian, but I've a fair idea. I paid in for seventeen years back home. Now they want thirty years for a basic pension, but I've heard that they're putting it up to thirty-five soon. Either way I'm going to get about half the basic pension."

"That's not much. What about your years teaching in Murcia before you came here?"

"Nine and a half years, ending fifteen years ago. I haven't a clue if they'll give me anything, but I'm not counting on it."

"And you're sixty now?" Brian asked, because Jack had let his last few birthdays slip quietly by.

"Yes, five to go."

The fact that it appeared that he would have to face those five years with little or no income hung like a cloud between the two men. Jack tried to lighten proceedings.

"The damnable thing is that you don't know how long you're going to live. If I knew I was going to pop my clogs at, say, seventy-seven, I could make better calculations," he said with a laugh.

"You're a fit bugger, though, and you don't even drink much."

"No, perhaps I should hit the bottle and take up smoking again." He laughed again in an attempt to ease his friend's discomfiture.

"Have you much saved, if you don't mind me asking?"

"I don't and I have. I've still got a good few thousand in the bank, but, as I say, it's the long term that I'm worried about. I can't see myself back in England."

"No, of all of us here, you're the most settled. I remember when we first met and you started speaking. You sounded like a Spaniard talking Lancashire."

"I remember. I hadn't spoken much English for a while then." Jack chuckled at the thought.

"You still, don't, apart from with me."

"Well, you know me. I don't mind building swimming pools, but I don't particularly like talking about them."

"My Spanish is still rubbish and I doubt it'll get much better now. What do you talk about with Vicente, Salvador and the others?" Brian asked, more cheerful now that the subject of work had been dropped, and perhaps reassured because Jack had told him about his nest egg.

"Oh, all sorts of things. Spanish blokes, or at least the ones I get on with, don't tend to go on about... material things so much. We might start talking about politics, then move on to vegetables and finish up with, I don't know, our childhood or something."

"Deep stuff, eh?"

"Not really, just chatter."

"Well I get more than my fair share of materialist stuff when I talk to folk, but when people start a new life somewhere it's what they're bound to talk about."

Yes, Jack thought, but not go on and on about houses, pools, cars and savings for year after year as if there were nothing more to life. "I guess you need to put up with it to be in the know about any work that might come up," he said, though he knew that Brian's conversation rarely strayed far from mundane matters even when alone with him for hours on end. "I suppose I've never been much use at drumming up trade."

"You got us that job doing Salvador's roof."

"A one-off. Anyway, I'll be off to the market now. Don't worry about me and just let me know when the next big job comes up. I'll keep my eyes open too. The locals know you're a good builder, you know."

"Yes, but I can't beat Martínez and company on price. If you want Liz to look anything up for you on the computer just let me know, or pop round."

"Thanks, I will."

Brian began to push himself to his feet, furrowed his brow, and dropped back into his chair.

"You know, if the worst comes to the worst you could sell the house and rent somewhere. The money would keep you for years and if you ever did need to go back home you might as well go back skint because they wouldn't do anything for you until you were practically penniless."

"This is home to me now, Brian. This village and my house. I can't see myself anywhere else. I'll just have to put my thinking cap on. See you soon."

Jack walked down the street feeling oddly relieved that his days of working for Brian appeared to be over. Both men knew that Jack, or at least his back, wasn't up to the really heavy work any longer, and large projects were precisely when the heavy work, such as lifting and placing concrete beams, was required. The fact that Brian's son, Josh, had just finished school might be another decisive factor, too, he reflected, as he couldn't imagine what else the strapping but rather dim lad would do if not work for his dad.

The only thing that really disturbed Jack about their meeting had been Brian's final comment about selling the house. He knew Brian well and him standing up, having a brainwave, and sitting down again hadn't fooled him for a minute. He knew that Brian had planned to offer up that suggestion at some point, but why? Time would tell, no doubt.

Deciding to give the market a miss, he walked past the church into the square and entered Julio's bar. The din of chatter didn't lessen as he walked along the bar to his usual corner, but most of the dozen or so men who sat or stood at the bar greeted him briefly. He placed his folded paper on the counter and pulled up a stool.

"*Qué tal*, Jack? What's it going to be? asked Julio, the short, stout, often curmudgeonly owner who had taken over the running of the bar from his father some thirty years earlier. He refurbished the place every ten years and they said that each time he did it he became a little grumpier, just like his father had.

"*Buenos días,* Julio. Toast with tomato and oil, and a coffee," he replied, having learnt long ago that saying *por favor* and *gracias* to Julio annoyed rather than pleased him, probably because he rarely used the words himself.

Julio popped the two halves of a baguette into the toaster and brought Jack his usual coffee, a *cortado*, strong with just a touch of milk. "What's new, Jack?"

"Nothing much. Just pottering on," he said, fearing that anything he told Julio of his current dilemma might be around the village by lunchtime. He unfolded his paper and glanced at the usual headlines about political strife and corruption and wondered why he had bought it. The men nearest to him were talking about football, just for a change, even though the season hadn't even started.

The main reason Jack preferred the corner at the end of the bar was that he had his back to the television, which was on all day, every day. On his rare evening visits he would feign interest in the inevitable football match, but only out of politeness. He didn't have a television at home, preferring the radio, music or, better still, silence, but he was long resigned to the fact that rare was the bar in Spain where the television wasn't on. There was some kind of morning chat show on now, but no-one was paying the slightest attention to it. Jack was amused by how interminable the adverts had become and the fact that nobody seemed to mind. He sometimes wished he'd been born a hundred years earlier and, by some quirk of fate, ended up in the village. Television, cars and computers; they could keep them all.

When Jaime, a young joiner who was making a go of it in the local area, dropped the subject of Real Madrid's latest signing and began talking about work he pricked up his ears.

"The new English couple who bought old Amador's place out past the cemetery had me out there yesterday to give them a quote for some work," he said to Federico, the plumber.

"What state is the place in now?" Federico asked.

"There's work to do, but he seems to have got stuck into it himself. I saw a lot of plastic tubing on the porch, so there might not be anything for you there."

"And you?"

"Oh, a couple of doors and some shelves, but he pulled a face when I told him how much," said Jaime, tapping a cigarette out of his packet.

"The last few new ones have all been a bit handy. Jack!" Federico called across the bar when Jaime had gone to the doorway to smoke. "What's the story with the English out past the cemetery?"

"I haven't a clue, Fede. Are they from Yorkshire?" he asked, pronouncing the county as a Spaniard would.

"God knows. I'm only assuming they're *ingleses*, because they usually are. Have they called you and Brian yet?"

"Not me, but I think they might have spoken to Brian. He's the boss."

"Hmm, piles of tubing," said Federico, thinking aloud. "He'll botch it up and then call me in to fix it." He took a cigarette packet from his shirt pocket and went to join Jaime at the door.

Jack ate the toast that Julio had set down in front of him and thought what a chump he had been all these years. Of Brian and himself, who was the one who had access to the local grapevine? He was. Who saw the other builders and tradesmen week in and week out? He did. Brian had said that his Spanish was rubbish, but it wasn't that, it was non-existent. After fourteen years he couldn't string a sentence together and probably knew a couple of hundred words. True, Brian was round like a shot when new Brits moved in, but *he* was the one who could have sussed out the state of their properties before the removal van reached the door.

Indolence, that's what it was. With his two hundred or so Euros coming in every week he hadn't given a thought to the future, and now look where he was? Facing the prospect of selling his house and counting down the years until he would have to return to England, cap in hand. Or would his money last him out till he died? His parents had both passed away in their early seventies, but people lived longer these days, especially healthy ones.

"Julio, a glass of wine, *por favor*."

"Sí, señor," he replied in mock deference, fishing a bottle of white from the fridge. "You look thoughtful there, Jack."

"Oh, just wondering what to have for lunch."

"Of course." Julio took off his glasses and polished them with a napkin. "I saw Brian at Ramón's the other day, loading up with sand and cement."

"Ah."

"His son was with him."

"Right."

"Brian was showing him how to get a bag of cement onto his shoulder."

"Well, he'll need to know how to do that," said Jack, smiling.

"What'll you have for lunch then?"

"What? Oh, fish, I think."

"Talk to Martínez."

"What about? Fish?"

"Ha, no. You know what about."

"Hmm."

When two men of few words get together, their conversations tend to go like that, Jack thought, but a lot could be said in a few words. Julio was reputed to have a heart of gold, albeit a well-concealed one, and if any man knew the state of play in the local labour market it was him. Still, approaching Martínez, Brian's up-and-coming rival, seemed like treachery. On the other hand, Brian setting his son to work without warning him wasn't exactly cricket either.

Perhaps I should wait until Brian gets his next big project, Jack thought. If he doesn't call me then, I'll know it's over. A shame, but inevitable. Family first, after all. Brian's a good bloke and it's probably embarrassment more than anything else that's kept him from speaking up. Still, it was strange of him to suggest me selling the house. Sounded like someone else speaking through him. His wife, Liz? She's a funny one. I've never been able to work her out. Wait and see, that's what I'll have to do.

"Martínez usually comes in after lunch on Saturdays," said Julio, interrupting his reverie.

"Hmm, perhaps I'll have meat today, after all."

"Suit yourself."

"Thanks anyway. What do I owe you?"

"Oh, three."

Jack paid and was taking his leave of the other men at the bar when Julio ushered him back.

"I'd have fish today, if I were you, Jack."

"Why's that?"

"It's good brain food."

2

"I told her to tell him to tell him," said Denise as she lugged herself up the pool steps, water cascading from her voluminous body.

"What's that, dear?" asked her husband Les from the sunbed.

"Jack, you know. I told Liz to tell Brian to put the idea of selling his house into his head like you told me to." She towelled herself briefly before easing herself onto the sunbed next to her husband's.

"Do you think she did?"

"I'm *sure* she told Brian, but whether he had the guts to mention selling the house, I don't know. I mean, the last I heard he hadn't even told the old duffer that he wouldn't be needing him much longer now that Josh'll be starting to work with him."

"I don't think Jack's much older than us, dear."

"He seems older, being so serious, and he's got no friends; apart from Brian, I suppose."

"He knocks about a lot with the Spanish."

"They don't count, and what does he do with himself stuck out in the country all the time?"

"Enjoy the view. That's why I want to buy his house," said Les, picking up an old copy of *The Sun* and putting it down again.

"What wrong with this one? She pointed vaguely in the direction of the smart five bedroom bungalow to their left.

"Poor view. No future. You know I want to start thinking about investing. We'll buy him out and either put another storey on the house – Brian says it's well built – or knock it down and build a new one. It's got the best view of any place I've seen round here and Néstor says that the land in the valley will come up for sale soon, once the old chap who owns it pops his clogs."

"Néstor? That young lawyer who you brought here once? He looks like a crook."

"That's why I like him," said Les with a chuckle. "He's doing well for himself down in Alicante, but he always keeps an eye on things round here. If we're not careful, he'll snap up Jack's house and then where will we be?"

"Here, in this lovely house with a heated pool."

"There's no future here, dear. It's done us for two years and it'll do for a couple more, but I want *that* view. I want to sit there and watch the houses I build in the valley make money for us."

"I thought we'd come here to retire, Les. When you sold the haulage firm you said we were set up for life."

"And we are, but I can't just sit here day after day," he said, patting his paunch. "I've got to stay active."

"Take up jogging or something then."

"Ha, that's a good one. Be a dear and fetch me a beer."

"In a minute, I'm just thinking. What do you mean about building houses? I thought the housing market was shot to bits."

"What goes down comes up, dear, but whatever I decide to do I want Jack's house."

"How do you know he's skint anyway?"

"Stands to reason. Old car sat there gathering dust. The clothes he wears. Cycling round everywhere. Still a few years to retirement, I'd say, and no more work. He'll have to go back home, like all the other failures."

"Brian might still find some work for him."

"No, he won't."

"How do you know?"

"Because I'm… we're, going to buy that little old house that I showed you at the edge of the village and I'm going to get Brian to do it up, on one condition." Les closed his eyes. He loved to tantalise his wife and anybody else who would listen to him.

"What condition?"

"That he doesn't use Jack. By the time he's finished the work his lad will have got into the swing of things and there'll be no looking back."

"You're a devil, you are, Les."

"I didn't build up a fleet of seventy lorries by being Mr Nice, did I?"

"Still, it doesn't seem right."

"All's fair in love and business. How about that beer?"

Denise swung her hefty legs off the sunbed and pushed herself to her feet. "I suppose I could invite Liz and Brian to lunch on Saturday."

"That's my girl."

* * *

Three miles to the south, on the other side of the village, Jack sat in possession of the view that the wily Brummie, Les, coveted so, but the fact that it was his fourth consecutive day without working was playing on his mind. Not that he'd been idle. There was hardly a weed on his land and all his neat rows of tomatoes, lettuces, peppers, melons and watermelons were well watered. He had picked a box of plums which he'd give to Salvador when he came round later for lunch. He had even washed his fifteen year old Seat Ibiza and driven it down to the road and back to keep the battery charged. The house was spotless and he had swept and mopped the covered porch before making himself a cup of tea and taking it out to the table in the shade.

He looked down the valley at the fields planted mostly with olive and almond trees. He saw old Pedro on his tractor, ploughing as usual, and waved. The old man was too far away to see him and Jack marvelled at his tenacity. He must be pushing eighty now, he thought, and struggles to walk from his car to the bar, but he never misses a day's ploughing, not even on Sundays. Mind you, he's got enough fields to keep him busy, but what'll happen when he goes? His eldest, Pedro too, is the only one still farming. The other three have all left the village and rarely visit. Perhaps young

Pedro will buy them out, but he's pushing sixty and spends more time in the bar in a week than his father does in a year.

"They don't make 'em like they used to," he said aloud, causing the stray cat that was sunning itself on the low porch wall to prick up its ears. "I'll get you a bit of something in a minute," he told the black tomcat. He wasn't especially fond of cats and fed them titbits only occasionally as he didn't want them to take over the place. He thought about getting another dog. Toby, a springer spaniel that he'd acquired in his first year in the house, had died just over a year ago and it was high time he started thinking about getting a new puppy. A dog was company – mostly silent company – and gave you a reason to go for good long walks. He'd ask around.

He went inside and started preparing the paella. As it was only for two he used his smaller paella pan on the biggest gas ring. While the chicken was sizzling in the olive oil he bought from the local cooperative he chopped up the onion, peppers and tomatoes. After taking out the browned chicken pieces he popped the vegetables in, followed by a couple of sliced garlic cloves, before sprinkling on some paprika, mixed herbs and saffron powder. After a few minutes he put the chicken back in and added water from the kettle that had just boiled. Once he had stirred it all thoroughly he left it to simmer for ten minutes before taking out the chicken, pouring in the rice, and giving it one quick stir. Ten minutes later he put the chicken back in, gave the pan a shake, and went outside while the rice slowly cooked, confident that the amount of water was just right. His paellas were nothing fancy, but after much trial and error over the years they always came out pretty well. Making a bigger one required a little more attention to detail, but it had been a while since he had used the larger pan and the special paella burner.

Three was a big lunch party for Jack nowadays and occurred only when Salvador and Vicente both came. In the early days he'd had more people round, but the aimless chitchat that had ensued had bored him and he soon ceased to conform to that and other social norms, such as taking part in the village fiestas.

Every May for as long as anyone could remember the village had celebrated a three-day-long Moors and Christians fiesta and in his second year of residence he had been badgered into taking part. He had been drafted into the Moors' *comparsa* and remembered vividly the evening of the grand procession when they had blacked their faces and donned fancy costumes that they hired from a place in Elda. They had marched along in three rows, very slowly and bobbing from side to side, to the beat of the village band, and the route from the edge of the village to the church had seemed to take forever.

"Did you not *feel* it, Jack?" one member of his *comparsa* had asked him later at the dance in the square.

"Feel what, Luis?"

"The passion, the feeling that you were in their shoes as they marched all over Spain a thousand years ago."

"Well, yes, a bit," he had said, untruthfully. He doubted that the Arab invaders marched with brass bands and was amused by the fact that Luis, who worked in the country, hated the Moroccans who came to pick the olives every autumn, claiming that they pushed wages down. "We should get some of the Moors who come to work here to take part," he had added.

"Pah, they're not the real thing, the sneaky bastards. In any case, they don't drink, so they wouldn't enjoy it."

The following year Jack had timed his trip to England to visit his ailing mother to coincide with the fiestas and hadn't been asked to take part since. These reminiscences brought his mind back to his current situation. Perhaps if he had taken part in the fiestas all these years more work would have come his way. Not unless he had hustled for it, and that wasn't his way. No, he had put all his eggs in Brian's basket, so to speak, and he was too old to start asking round now. Why then Julio's insistence that he speak to Martínez? Perhaps there was something in it, but he baulked at the idea of approaching that brash man who was young enough to be his son.

Shortly after he had turned off the gas and covered the paella with a sheet of newspaper he heard Salvador's car coming up the track. As the well-used diesel saloon came to a halt on the gravelled area in front of the house he walked down the three porch steps to greet his friend. Salvador took off his tie and draped it over the passenger seat before closing the door and walking jauntily towards the house. He was a short, rotund man of forty-five who despite not having much time or inclination to exercise seemed to have boundless energy.

"Hola, Salva, you're just in time." The two men shook hands and half embraced.

"*Qué tal*, Jack? I'm starving. I've just driven back from Denia and what a waste of time that was."

"Why's that?"

"Oh, they've got me working on a housing development there that's never going to happen."

"But they'll pay you, won't they?"

"Oh, yes. That's the good thing about working for town councils. They almost always pay, eventually."

Salvador was a lawyer who worked all over the Valencian region, mainly on housing-related matters and usually for PSOE-led town councils. During the ten years he had served as a village councillor for the Spanish Socialist Party he had made a lot of useful contacts and until the property crash of 2008 had been going from strength to strength. Since then he had employed his considerable ingenuity to keep ticking over until things picked up.

"Are things picking up yet, Salva?" Jack asked him as they entered the house.

"Hmm…" He pulled a comic face and moved his head from side to side. "They're not getting any worse."

Salvador refused to let things get him down and his sense of humour had helped him battle through several tough years. He drove tens of thousands of kilometres a year, to towns as far afield as Morella in Castellón, in an effort to keep his and his wife and two young children's bodies and souls together. Jack thought Salvador's wife, Chelo, rather silly and didn't see much of her or the children. Salvador was shockingly honest about his marriage.

"There I was, an ugly little chap of thirty-three, and along came a pretty young thing ten years younger than me who saw the brilliant man behind this homely face," he had once said during his second post-dinner whisky. "She's not the brightest spark in the world, I know, and I won't deny that my earning potential might have been a major factor in her choice, but she keeps me off this stuff," he had said, lifting his glass. "She's given me two fine children too, with their father's brains and their mother's looks, so who am I to complain?"

Salvador had been similarly blunt when he saw how difficult Jack found it to converse with her. "No more of these little family get-togethers for us Jack," he had said after a particularly trying afternoon at his house in the village. "Family's family and friends are friends and I'll spare you the ordeal from now on."

"No, no, it's been fine," Jack had protested.

"Don't worry, she doesn't think much of you either. She wonders why you don't work more, and talk more. It'll be tête-à-tête for us from now on, unless the dancing policeman joins us."

Although both were from the village, Salvador and Vicente, due to their ten year age difference, hadn't really known each other until they met through Jack. Since then they had become firm friends and Salvador, unlike Jack, had been to a couple of Latin dancing sessions with Vicente in Monóvar, until Chelo had put a stop to that.

"Is that old lawman Vicente coming today?" asked Salvador while Jack uncorked a bottle of red wine.

"No, I called him but he's on the late shift."

Jack removed the newspaper and they both ate from the paella pan, leaving their chicken bones and olive stones on the same plate.

"What are you working on at the moment?" Salvador asked.

"Nothing."

"Nothing? Has Brian not got much on?"

"I don't really know, but he hasn't got anything for me. I think our partnership might be over now that his lad's old enough to work."

Salvador put down his fork and looked at Jack. "That's bad. Did he give you any warning?"

"No, probably too embarrassed."

"Funny folk the English. What will you do?"

"Let's eat, then I'll tell you my predicament."

After Jack had cleared and wiped the table they decided to have coffee in the shade of the porch. Jack took out the tray while Salvador trotted over to his car and returned with a bottle of brandy.

"*Gran Duque de Alba*," said Jack, reading the label. "This is a good one."

"Given to me by a councillor in Játiva, to make up for how little they're paying me, I think," he said with a snort of laughter.

"It's too good to go in the coffee. I'll get some glasses."

When he returned Salvador had taken his shirt off and was enjoying the coolest temperature since May. "Summer will soon be over, thank God. Now, Jack, drink a glass of this stuff and tell me what's on your mind."

Jack filled Salvador in on the state of his finances and pension prospects as accurately as he could. When he had finished Salvador nodded thoughtfully and sipped his coffee.

"It's bad, but it's not so bad," he said.

"No?"

"Just think about all the people in the Third World and how they live."

"Yes, well, I'm not comparing myself to those poor folk, but I don't want to end up back in England."

"England's not so bad. I spent a weekend in London once."

"Accrington's not London, Salva, though I wouldn't fancy that place much either."

"No, I guess it wouldn't suit you. Anyway, as I say, things don't look so bad to me. You have to look at your resources."

"Well, I've told you what I have."

"I don't just mean money, I mean *your* resources."

"Meaning?"

"Meaning what you're capable of doing. You weren't always a builder's labourer, were you?"

"Well, no. I used to work in an office, and then the teaching in Murcia."

"Right, well, I suppose things have changed a lot in offices these days, what with computers and all."

"Yes, we used them back then, but not the internet."

"What about teaching?"

"Teaching English? Well, I guess I still remember how to do that. In Murcia I used to teach groups of ten or twelve, from young kids up to adults."

"Why have you never done that here, Jack?"

"To tell you the truth I was pretty fed up of it towards the end; that and city life. That's why I left and moved up here. I'd realised that I didn't like to be around so many people. I took it easy for a year, though I did a lot of work on the land here, and then I started working for Brian."

Salvador took his cigarettes from his shirt pocket and lit one. "There's nothing to stop you looking for English classes here; you know, kids who are struggling at school, or adults who fancy having a go. With Spain being in such a bad way English is a passport out of here for some people."

"I'd feel daft teaching kids at my age, though I guess I could cope with adults, one-to-one."

"There you are then. That's one possible source of income, but I think you could do a lot more."

"Such as?"

"Well, people like you here. They like and respect you and consider you almost one of themselves. They don't really think of you as a foreigner. That's one side of it. How do you get on with the British?"

"I don't really mix with them too much. I'll always stop for a chat if I see people in the village, but they probably think I'm a bit standoffish. I never see them socially, not even at Christmas and New Year when they tend to get together, some of them."

"Right, so you're not first on their party lists, but do they trust you?" Salvador asked, refilling their brandy glasses.

"Oh, I think so. Yes, I'd say they trust me."

"Trust, yes," Salvador said, sipping his brandy and appearing to examine the wooden beams above his head. He looked at Jack. "I'll tell you something about myself now."

"Go on."

"But I'm not... showing off. When I was a village councillor people soon saw that I didn't take bribes. When I got to know a lot of people at PSOE conferences in Alicante and Valencia I started making contacts for my work. They probably thought, 'Here's another pushy young lawyer on the make,' but when anyone showed any real interest I said to them, 'Look, first of all check me out. Speak to the other councillors in the village – the PP and IU ones too, not just my colleagues – and you'll see that I'm a man you can trust.' Mind you, they didn't all like that," he said, laughing.

"Why not?" asked Jack, wondering where all this was going.

"Because some people on some councils *want* a crooked lawyer. Anyway, the point I'm making is that trust can get you a long way. If it hadn't been for the property crash I'd be a wealthy man by now. As it is I've pulled through the worst of it while a lot of other lawyers have had to practically give it up. Enough about me. Let's talk about you now."

"What about me?" Jack pushed his empty brandy glass out of Salvador's reach.

"The people here trust you. The foreigners trust you. You know about building and quite a bit about houses in general. Think about it."

"I'm thinking and I think I know what you're going to suggest. Trust is one thing, but… communication is another. I'm a quiet man, Salva, and I haven't got much push. I can still work all day long, but get me in a group of people and I can't leave quickly enough."

"You're a quiet man, so you go about your business quietly. You quietly speak to everyone in the village, directly or indirectly, and quietly tell them that if they have any property to sell that they speak to you first. Then, when just about everybody is aware of your new role, you speak quietly to the foreigners who you come across and tell them that you're dealing with practically every property that's for sale in and around the village, so if they know anybody who wants to buy they should come to you first if they want to avoid paying a whacking great commission on top of the house price. You'll have to advertise too, of course, but we'll come to that later."

Jack reached for the bottle and poured himself another slug of brandy. He knew Salvador's fast and furious way of talking well, but had never had to assimilate anything quite like this before.

"Me selling houses? I just can't see it. I mean, what about all the paperwork and legal stuff? I haven't a clue."

"Can't you think of anyone you know who could deal with that side of things?"

"Only you, but you're too busy to bother with that."

"Ha! I wish I was. I'd love to get some work closer to home and I could probably undercut whoever people use now."

"Isn't there a lawyer called Néstor from the village? I hear talk of him sometimes."

"Bad things, probably. He's based mainly in Alicante now, but he may have some dealings with Martínez the so-called builder."

"I'd been meaning to ask you about Martínez. You know, Julio at the bar was insinuating that I should have a word with him. He knows that Brian's son has started work now, you see."

"Hmm, Martínez has quite a bit of work on just now, and he'll get more. My guess is that he wants you on board so he can use you to get in with the English."

"Do you think so?"

"Why else? He can get workers half your age if he needs more men. Don't go near him. He's a shoddy worker, by all accounts, and if he's hand in glove with Néstor, as I assume he is because they're made for each other, it'll make things easier for us."

"Why's that?"

"Remember what we were saying about trust? No-one here trusts that pair, especially Néstor. You just need to point out, subtly, to the foreigners that neither of them is trustworthy. I can give you some gossip about both of them that you can slip into the conversation." He lit another cigarette and blew the smoke to one side.

Jack stirred his neglected coffee and took a sip. "I'll have to think about all this, Salva. It's not something I'd have ever thought of doing. The English classes might be a better bet."

"There's nothing to stop you doing that too. The thing is to make a start on the house selling idea. Just put the word out in the village that people ought to tell you if they have anything to sell." Salvador sipped his brandy and flicked ash over the side of the porch. "You could charge them a flat fee of, say, a thousand euros, at first."

"Marta won't be pleased when she hears about it, or her dad, Marco."

"Too bad. He's another rogue and should stick to baking bread."

"Won't they accuse me of working illegally?"

"Probably, but you won't be working, will you? You'll just be bringing interested parties together. When you start approaching possible buyers, you tell them a couple of stories about Néstor, like the scandal in San Vicent del Raspeig that he was involved in. I've got a newspaper clipping at home somewhere. Then tell them you know a trustworthy lawyer who knows everything there is to know about housing matters." Salvador pointed to himself and pulled a face of mock surprise.

"I'll need to think about it. I don't like treading on people's toes."

"Where is it you're from in England?"

"Accrington, in Lancashire, in the north."

"What's it like?"

"It's... well, I haven't been back for a few years, but it's... I guess you'd call it post-industrial." He thought about the beer-drinking loiterers who had been much in evidence on his last trip home to see his sister, but also about the good folk who lived there. "It's not a bad town really."

"And the weather?"

Jack looked down at his brown hands. "Now it might be all right, but most of the year it's terrible."

"When you have doubts, think of Accrington."

3

While Denise was putting the finishing touched to lunch Les was scooping a few dead flies from the pool. He looked up at the ragged hedge of cypress trees that bordered the southern edge of his small plot of land and scowled. He had had the trees planted to obscure the view of a neighbouring house – a scruffy one owned by natives – but the flat location of his property meant that the view wasn't much better to the east or west either. To the north it was passable because of the distant hills, but it wasn't much use to him as there was no porch on that side of the house and it wouldn't have got the sun anyway.

No, he'd rushed into buying the land and building the house and now regretted it. He doubted that many people who had owned a business as successful as his had to put up with such a poor view. A life of toil just for this! He heard a vehicle pull into the driveway and walked around the house to greet his guests, his sandals scraping along over the immaculate gravel. His scowl disappeared as the back of the van came into view and he greeted Brian and Liz heartily.

"There you are. No Josh?"

"No, he says he's too tired to move after working all day yesterday," said Liz, a good-looking blonde woman some years younger than and about half the weight of her husband who Les thought had a touch of madness in her large blue eyes.

"He'll soon get used to it," said Brian, a bottle of cava in each of his huge hands.

"Hello, you two," called Denise from the front doorway in the singsong voice she reserved for social occasions.

Les wondered if you put his wife and Brian on either end of a seesaw who would hit the ground first. There wasn't much in it and he thought he'd read somewhere that muscle weighed more than fat, so Brian might edge it, but he had more important things on his mind than his wife's weight, and he could hardly talk.

"You all go round to the terrace and I'll bring some drinks out," trilled Denise before disappearing into the house.

"The garden's looking lovely," said Liz as Denise poured out the sangría.

"Yes, a little man from the village comes in twice a week. Can't understand a word of English, but he does more or less what I tell him," Denise said before popping a cheese and onion crisp into her mouth.

"I wish we lived in the country instead of in that big old house in the village," said Liz, trapping a single peanut between her long, bright red fingernails.

"It's a lovely house, Liz, after all the work that Brian's done on it," said Denise.

"Oh, I know," she replied, patting her husband's arm absently. "But the village can be… claustrophobic, and it's murder when those noisy fiesta are on."

Les cleared his throat. "Well, we all aspire to better things, don't we? And it's never too late to get them if you take your opportunities."

"Jack's not planning on selling," said Brian rather abruptly, shaking his head at the sangría jug.

"Liz, can you give me a hand with the plates, please? asked Denise.

"I'll be in in a minute, love," Liz said, fixing her eyes on her husband. Denise remained seated and refilled the glasses.

"It's normal that his first reaction is to say no," said Les, looking only at Brian and smiling. "If I offer him a little bit over the going price he might change his mind. Thanks for asking him anyway, Brian. How did you slip it into the conversation?"

"I don't know, I just asked him if he'd ever thought about selling," Brian said. He hadn't told his wife about Jack's revelations regarding his money worries and he certainly wasn't going to share his long-time friend's woes with this pushy Brummie. It had been hard enough to tell Jack that he didn't have any work for him and only the thought of his wife's reaction made him slip the question into the conversation. Why Liz thought so much of these two he did not know.

Denise went inside to fetch the lunch and Liz followed her. During the meal of steak and kidney pie, chips and vegetables, washed down with a bottle of red wine, they talked mainly of the relative merits of eateries within driving distance. They agreed that the Indian restaurant at La Murada was great value for money and Denise said that the one in Fortuna was just as good. Brian mentioned the new restaurant in the village that they hoped to visit soon.

"Spanish, isn't it? We don't really do Spanish food," said Les. "Do we, Denise?"

"Too oily for us. All that oil can't be good for you. Are you all ready for dessert?"

By the time they had eaten and praised Denise's homemade sticky toffee pudding and custard they were all too full to speak, so while Denise put the plates in the dishwasher Les prepared a strong pot of coffee and moved their guests' bottles of cava from the freezer to the fridge.

"There's a little house in the village that I want you to have a look at for me," Les said to Brian on finishing his first cup of coffee. "It's at the end of the street where that scruffy bar is."

"That'll be Mario's bar."

"I didn't see a name."

"No, the sign fell to bits a few years ago and he didn't bother replacing it. It's a real spit and sawdust place. Do you mean the house at the end that hasn't been lived in for a while?"

"That's the one. I asked in that Spanish estate agent's and she says it's going dirt cheap," he said, before lifting his forefinger and lumbering into the house.

"I'm thinking of buying that house," he said as he appeared through the patio doors with a bottle of cava and four glasses.

"What on earth for, dear?" asked Denise with well-feigned surprise. Her acting skills had been useful to Les at more than one work-related dinner party back in their last home in Edgbaston.

"Because it's there," he said, before laughing loudly. The effects of the coffee, the appearance of the sparkling wine and this jovial eruption helped to drive away the post-lunch drowsiness that Les now wished to dispel.

"Well if it's there it can stay there," said Denise. She tutted and shook her head. "What do you want with an old place like that?"

"Don't worry, it's not for us, dear. No, this retirement lark doesn't suit me too well after all. I shan't get back into haulage – I don't even know the word for lorry in Spanish – but I need to do something to keep myself active. I intend to buy that house, do it up, and sell it. That way I'll start learning about the ins and outs of the property business over here. What do you think, Brian?"

"To be honest, Les, I wouldn't buy it. However cheap it is, it'll still need a lot spending on it and the market hasn't picked up again yet."

"But it will. It's bound to. What goes down comes up, ha ha! That house is just a start. If things go well I'll be investing a lot more money in the years to come. Now, do you want to do it up for me? You and Josh?"

Brian took a sip of cava in order to hide his eagerness. He cleared his throat and exhaled slowly. "Well, it's a big job, but it'd be just the thing to teach Josh what building's all about. I'd be able to give Jack some work too, which would be great. I felt awful about telling him that I probably wouldn't have anything for him now that Josh is starting."

His delight at the prospect of a real project was tempered by the recollection of the fact that he hadn't had the heart to tell Jack that his son was going to replace him. Les noticed his ruffled brow and topped up their glasses.

"How long would it take to do the house up?" asked Denise, sensing that her husband needed time to think.

"Oh, that depends on how much needs doing and how thorough the restoration is going to be," said Brian. "A couple of months, I would say."

"If a job's worth doing, it's worth doing well," said Les, hauling himself upright in his wicker chair. "What I'm really interested in, looking further ahead, is the land in the valley to the south of the village. I believe it's all owned by one man and that he'll probably be… retiring soon."

"That'll be old Pedro's property," said Brian. "He'll not sell while he's got a breath of life in him. Jack knows him well. He's one of the old school. Tied to the land, so to speak."

"As I say, it's a long-term project, but I can see that land divided up into big lots with a really great house and pool on each of them."

"That's ambitious," said Liz, looking from Les to Brian and back again.

"He's like that," said Denise, patting her husband's knee. "I want him to take it easy, but I know what he's like." She topped up the glasses and took the empty bottle into the house.

"I'm going to speak to an up-and-coming lawyer I know called Néstor," said Les. "He speaks good English and although he works away he knows everything that's going on around here. I'm hoping that by the time you and Josh finish doing up the house in the village I'll have bought at least some of that land in the valley; enough to build a really great house on, a kind of show house. Now, Brian, do you feel capable of building a house like that from scratch?"

"Oh, I've got the knowhow all right, but I'd have to hire more men. I could do with having someone on the job who knows the trade and speaks good Spanish though, to arrange plant hire and suchlike."

"Well, whichever architect I hire is going to have to speak good English for a start. I'll want to know exactly where my money's going! How's your Spanish?"

"Well…"

"It's quite good really," said Liz. "And Josh is fluent."

"I know most of the building-related words and it's true that Josh speaks like a native, but I'm not sure that the building game is for him. He's struggled so far, which is normal, but he's going to have to show more enthusiasm if he's going to get anywhere. It's a tough game and not for everyone. Jack's Spanish is brilliant. He'll be a godsend."

"More cava, folks," said Denise with exquisite timing. She refilled the glasses and took her seat.

"Remember that I'm thinking in the long-term though, Brian," said Les. "Jack's getting on a bit and I want some young blood involved in the project."

"I think-"

"In five years or so I want to really retire," he went on. "By then I want all the houses in the valley to be finished – at least six or seven of them – and I want one of them to be yours." He smiled at Liz before looking into Brian's eyes.

"Oh, Brian, that would be something really worth working for," Liz said with a wide-eyed, almost maniacal smile at her husband. "A house with a pool in the country! By then it'll be time for you to think about retiring too."

"It's all very exciting," said Brian, the flatness of his voice not matching his words. He was waiting for the catch.

Les lifted his glass and proposed a toast. "To us and our country retreats." They all clinked glasses and drank. Les placed his empty glass on the table. "We'll be neighbours too, because I'm determined to buy that house off Jack, for a very fair price, of course. It'll overlook the project and it's got just the sort of view that I'm missing out here."

Brian twirled his glass on the table top and studied its contents. "Jack's house is something between you and him, Les, and I guess it's only a house, after all. I do want him with me on the restoration though, and he'll be invaluable when you start looking into buying Pedro's land. He knows him well. He knows most people in the village, in fact."

"No, Brian, Jack doesn't form part of my plans; not now and not later," said Les quietly. "I want you and Josh to do up the house in the village. Give another youngster a chance if you need more manpower. You and me are the only old 'uns we need on this venture," he concluded with a chuckle that Brian didn't reciprocate.

"But what's Jack going to do? He's still got five years to go until he retires," Brian said, looking at each of them in turn.

Only Les looked him in the eye. "I'm a businessman, Brian, and I've taken plenty of tough decisions over the years. I work on intuition and I just know that Jack's not right for the project. We're bound to rub some local people up the wrong way, that's inevitable, and from what I've heard Jack's too soft to be a part of it. If we offend any of the locals he might take their side and I can't afford to risk that. I've always run a tight ship and if you want to come aboard that's one of my conditions."

Brian's hands gripped the edge of the table, making it appear flimsy, and looked at Les beneath lowered brows. Liz brushed her leg against his and he relaxed his grip.

"So, Les," he began after closing and reopening his eyes. "The reason you don't want me to give Jack any work is because he doesn't form part of your long-term plans."

"That's right, Brian."

"Not because you want to force him to sell up."

Denise drew a sharp and very audible breath. "Oh, Brian, how can you think such a thing? Les will give him a very good price for his house; better than he'd get from anyone else. It would help rather than hinder his… retirement prospects, I'm sure."

"That house can't be worth more than €100,000 the way things are at the moment," said Les, who had had it surreptitiously valued two days previously. "I'll give him – and you can tell him this if you wish – €125,000 for it right now. That's a gift of twenty thousand quid. It'd take him a good while to earn that."

"But he just doesn't want to move, Les," said Brian, in as appealing a voice as he could muster.

"We all have to do things we don't like sometimes," said Liz, patting her husband's brawny forearm. "It's a very good offer," she added on noting the withdrawal of his arm.

"We'd better be off now," Brian said to his hosts. "Thanks for a lovely lunch." He stood up, smiled at Denise, nodded at Les, and walked down the terrace steps and around the house towards his van.

They listened to his footsteps growing fainter on the gravel. "Well?" Denise asked Liz.

"Better than I expected. You go ahead and buy that old house, Les, and I'll see to the rest."

"That's my girl, Lizzie."

4

Jack invited Vicente to lunch on his next day off, a Tuesday. Instead of making the lunch he just assembled the implements and ingredients he though his friend might need. Vicente would arrive early and loved cooking. When the small white car drew to a halt next to his own he went to greet him. After they had embraced Vicente held him at arm's length and looked at him playfully.

"You're looking younger and fitter than ever, Jack. It must be the country air."

"I'm fine. You're not looking too bad yourself. What's in the bag?"

Vicente opened the plastic bag to reveal a huge lobster sitting atop half a dozen artichokes. "I bought this beast in Monóvar yesterday. There are some shrimps in there somewhere too."

Jack nodded and smiled, hoping that the lobster would be dismantled during the cooking process. "It looks... tasty. I've got the rice and things out," he said, sure that rice would be required. Vicente prepared an ever-expanding variety of dishes, often quite experimental, but always with rice. He claimed that potatoes were a foreign import, being from the New World, and that pasta was little more than compressed bread.

While his friend made himself at home in the kitchen, Jack poured two glasses of white wine. Although Vicente wasn't as perceptive as Salvador, Jack valued his opinion just as much, but any serious talk would have to wait until the food was on the table. He watched with relief as Vicente took his biggest knife and sliced the lobster lengthways before cutting off the claws. Jack wasn't too fond of seafood and the smaller the pieces he had to tackle the better.

He soon saw that a simple lobster and shrimp paella was in the offing, rather than a bold new recipe. Vicente spoke little as he worked and Jack was happy to play the part of kitchen assistant. When the water was poured into the paella pan and the ingredients left to cook he asked Vicente how his Latin dancing was going.

"Ah, I'm improving all the time, or so my lovely teacher, Gabriela, says. She's from Venezuela and moves like a lynx."

Jack tried to imagine a lynx doing a tango, but failed. "That's over in Elda, isn't it?"

"Petrer, just next door. You should give it a go. The women outnumber the men by at least three to one. We're off to Valencia next Saturday to a big event there. You could come along."

"I've never had much rhythm."

"Me neither," said Vicente, and it was true that his rather stiff walk didn't suggest great dancing skills. "But if you practice enough you get better." He performed a few steps before spinning round and shimmying over to the kitchen top to get the rice.

"Any romance yet?" asked Jack as Vicente danced back with the bag of rice and a cup.

"Not yet, just friendship, but I'm in no hurry. I'm still enjoying my freedom from my once-beloved wife."

"Yes, perhaps it's best to be in no hurry," said Jack, remembering Carla, Vicente's petite, pretty, but rather possessive wife from whom he had divorced a few years earlier.

"What about you, Jack?"

"Oh, I'm still enjoying my… fourteen year sabbatical from the fair sex." He laughed quietly. "I think you could say I'm a confirmed bachelor by now."

"Never say never, Jack. You might want someone by your side in your old age." Vicente measured the rice into the pan, thus missing Jack's wince at the mention of old age. He had no problem with growing old as such, but was increasingly concerned about where he was going to be while he was doing it.

As soon as the paella was ready they took it outside to enjoy the relatively cool breeze on the porch. Twenty-seven degrees was the lowest midday temperature that the thermometer had registered for well over two months.

"Well, August is finally over," said Jack as he scraped a little lobster meat from the shell and mixed it with a forkful of rice.

"Thank God. It's no fun walking the beat when it's so hot. How does it taste?"

"Delicious, but I'll leave the claws to you. Weren't you going to get more office duties now that you've hit fifty-five?"

"I could, but I prefer to be out and about chatting to folk than stuck inside. What about you? Much work on with Brian?"

"Well, no. After we've eaten I'll tell you the whole story. How are Cristina and Olivia?" Jack asked, referring to Vicente's daughters.

"Cristina's still working at *El Corte Inglés* in Alicante and plans to marry next year. Olivia's gone to work in London."

"London? You didn't tell me that. Has she found a pharmacy job at last?"

"If only. No, she's working in a café and sharing a flat with a friend from university and other people. I spoke to her last night and she's glad just to be working."

"Yes, it's tough for the youngsters at the moment, though they say things are starting to pick up. More wine?" Jack lifted the empty bottle.

"Not for me."

After eating melon for dessert Jack put four in a bag for Vicente and made coffee.

"Salva brought this brandy the other day," he said as he slid the tray onto the round wooden table.

"How's the little devil doing?"

"Not too bad. He asked after you. We'll have to meet up when you get a free Saturday or Sunday."

"If Chelo lets him out."

"Yes." Jack chuckled. "I was telling him about my, er… predicament and we were trying to come up with some solutions."

Vicente poured the coffee into the cups and the brandy into the small glasses before speaking. "Now you can tell me."

Jack told him every detail of his economic situation and poor work prospects. He didn't mention Salvador's suggestions as he wanted to hear Vicente's objective opinion.

"It's bad," Vicente said after hearing Jack out.

"Yes."

"I told you you shouldn't have worked cash in hand for so long."

"I know, but what's done is done. What I need now are ideas."

Vicente stood up and walked the length of the tiled porch, looking at the house and at the land. "Why do anything?" he said on resuming his seat.

"What do you mean? I have to do *something*."

"Not necessarily. From what you've told me you have plenty to live on for the next five years."

"Not plenty, but enough, I guess."

"After that you'll get, what? Two-thirds of a pension?"

"If I'm lucky."

"Plenty to live on for a man of your simple tastes, I would say."

"No, it would be enough to survive on, just about, but what if something goes wrong? What if the house needs money spending on it? What if they bring in some new tax?"

"Well, you could always move to a smaller place."

Jack placed his coffee cup carefully onto the saucer and looked at his friend. "What makes you say that?"

"Nothing, really. It's just an option, that's all. Like the car, for instance. You don't really use it, do you?"

"Not much. But what you said about the house; have you been talking to anyone about me?"

"Not recently. Why? You look worried, Jack."

"No, it's nothing," he said, much relieved, before telling him about the conspiracy that he felt was afoot to get the house from him. "I'm not sure who wants it, but I have some ideas. I like it here and really can't see myself moving."

"No, sorry, it was just a hypothesis. I've been thinking about what I'm going to do and where I'm going to end up too, you see."

"What are your plans?"

"I want to retire at sixty. At sixty they'd definitely shove me in the office and I couldn't bear that. You know I'm renting that little flat at the moment, since Carla ended up with the house. Well, I want to buy a little place in the country, something like this but smaller, and grow my own vegetables like you do. If I keep my costs down I'll get by all right. My tastes are just as simple as yours, really, except that I'll need my car to go dancing."

"It sounds like a good idea, but you'll have a state pension and a police pension to look forward to."

"Yes, but I've got to buy the house yet, remember."

"That's true. Anyway, I appreciate your advice and I'll bear it in mind, but I really want to do something for the next few years. Salva suggested me giving English classes in the village."

"That's an idea," said Vicente, sucking on a plastic cigarette.

"He also thinks I could make money selling houses."

Vicente took the much chewed object from his mouth and picked up his brandy glass. The sun had begun to penetrate the porch and its reflection on his glasses prevented Jack from seeing his widening eyes. "*You* selling houses, Jack?"

"Why not?"

"Hmm, I just can't see it. It's not your style. It'd mean getting out there and talking to people for a start, and not just people you like."

"I know, but Salva was quite convincing and says that he'll take care of the legal side of things. At first all I have to do is get out and talk to people; ask them who's selling what. I'm sure I can manage that."

"Yes, I'm sure you'll find that out, but who's going to buy?"

"Well, I'll have to talk to all the British people too and see if they know anyone who's planning on moving out here. Then I guess I'll have to advertise."

"That'll cost money."

"Yes, and I haven't quite decided how to go about that yet."

"I can soon litter Monóvar with leaflets, if you make some of those. More brandy?"

"Just a tiny drop. Yes, I could write a leaflet and get someone to type it up for me. Thanks for the idea, and the offer. I'm no more convinced than you are, but I'll give it a try."

"Well, there's no harm in that, but, as I say, if you get rid of the car you'll be surprised by how little you can live on. I'm off home for a siesta now. Let me know if there's anything I can do."

"Thanks, Vicente. There is one small thing. When you're in the village I'd like you to keep your ears open and perhaps make a few enquiries about who is so set on buying my house."

"Ha, I've always fancied myself as a detective, but never really got the chance." He stood up. "Thanks for the melons and I'll report back to you as soon as I have some information."

Jack stood and they shook hands. Vicente performed a mock salute, turned, and left without another word, as he invariably did. He was superstitious about saying goodbye.

While he cleared up Jack pondered on Vicente's reaction to his bad news. He chuckled at his friend's lack of faith in his house selling abilities and thought that he might well be right. Salvador was a perennial optimist who had shown real grit over the last few years, whereas Vicente, potential dangers apart, had had a relatively easy and secure working life. It was good to have heard both his friends' opinions, but Vicente's suggestion of doing nothing at all had taken him aback. Even now the absence of his three weekly workdays with Brian was leaving something of a hole in his life.

Mind you, he had always managed to occupy himself on the other four days, and he was looking forward to picking up the parcel of second-hand books that ought to be waiting for him at the post office. A biography of Orwell, a large volume on the history of the American Indians, a couple of novels and a travel book by Wilfred Thesiger. Now there was a man, by all accounts, who really despised the modern world and spent years on end with nomads and other folk who still lived the same as they had for thousands of years. Thesiger wouldn't have sullied his hands selling houses, but then Thesiger had owned a house in Chelsea and had a private income. Still, he would read that one first.

"I'll pop in tomorrow morning, pick up the books and ride straight back," he said to the black tomcat which appeared to have taken up residence. No I won't, he thought. He would pick up the parcel first, but would not leave the village until he had spoken to at least ten people about his new venture. He frowned at the thought, but it wasn't so difficult really: 'Do you know anyone who wants to sell a house?' ten times over. In Julio's bar, Mario's bar and whoever he came across in the street. Perhaps the response would be poor and he could give up the idea. Maybe think about getting a few classes instead.

"Well, cat. I won't know until I've tried."

5

"Hola, Néstor? It's Martínez here. Adán Martínez."

"Martínez, fancy hearing from you. What can I do for you?"

It was curious that Martínez always preferred to be called by his surname, despite being the fifth of seven brothers and sisters. Some said it was because he wanted to be thought of as *the* Martínez and not just one of the clan.

"What's the story with this fat *inglés*? Les, I think he's called."

"Ah, *mi cliente*. I can't really disclose my client's business, you know."

"Come off it Néstor. We went to school together and he's just another damn *guiri*."

"We might have gone to school together, Adán, but I haven't seen you put any work my way yet. Why use lawyers from outside the village when you've got me?"

"Well, you're in Alicante now, aren't you?"

"Only thirty-five minutes away in my new car, Adán, and I love to see the old place, you know."

"Right, well, if I get anything worth your while, I'll let you know."

"You do that, Adán. *Hasta luego*."

"Wait. What about this Les then?"

"Hmm, if I tell you what he's planning to do and you end up doing it, I want *all* the legal work involved."

"You've got it, Néstor. Word of honour."

"Ha, one's word of honour doesn't go very far in my trade. Anyway, this Les wants to buy up old Pedro Poveda's land in the valley, either before or after he dies. He also wants –

he especially wants – the house and land of an *inglés* called Jack because it has a good view of the valley. He plans to rebuild the house and live there himself, to watch over his empire, I suppose."

"The English and their damn views!" said Martínez. "The cheap houses I could have restored for them if they'd only had good views."

"I know. They are obsessed with views. I don't think old Poveda will ever sell, and knowing that family I doubt that we'll see him under the earth for a while yet. I told the *inglés* that he was very old and quite ill, of course, and that he should make every effort to secure Jack's property as soon as possible."

"Right, well, thanks for telling me, Néstor, but it doesn't look too promising after all. Especially considering the way the housing market is."

"On the contrary. You have to take a long-term view of things. Remember that he's planning to sell the houses he builds to his compatriots. Although he's English I don't think he's stupid. He's obviously wealthy and seems sure that houses down there – luxury houses with pools – will sell. He knows his countrymen better than we do."

"That's true, Néstor. Perhaps there's something in it. Does he have a builder in mind for the houses?"

"He mentioned an *inglés* called Brian, but from what he tells me he's small fry. A development of those characteristics would be beyond him, I think."

"But not beyond me, Néstor. I'm expanding all the time."

"When the time comes we can discuss these things. I have a lot of influence over this Les and I'm sure he will use the builder I suggest. All this is in the future – hopefully the not too distant future – but the essential thing right now is to secure this man Jack's house. The fat *inglés* is only interested in Poveda's land if he can get the house on the hill."

"But why is that so important?"

"I told you, the view. He's quite old and is clearly not planning to embark on this project out of necessity. If he cannot have his view he won't go ahead. We must have the other Englishman's house."

"You mean the fat man must have it?"

"Not necessarily. Whoever gets the house holds the key to the whole business. Why, if that house were mine I would squeeze as much as 200,000 out of Les for it. Also, if he likes it so much it stands to reason that it must hold a special attraction for other English people too."

"I guess so. And this Jack?" asked Martínez. "What's he like?"

"A quiet man, well-liked in the village, I believe, not least because he speaks *castellano*, unlike most of the others. He's attached to the house, they say, but every man has his price."

"Well, let's hope that this Les buys it soon. Then we could have a word with old Poveda."

"Better to leave that side of things to me, Adán, but don't worry; if this thing comes off we will both make a *lot* of money. Keep in touch."

"I will, and thanks."

Martínez hung up the phone feeling that he was one step ahead of the canny Néstor Puig. The lawyer had told him little more than he already suspected. He knew for a fact that Néstor had already made overtures to old Poveda regarding the land and had been soundly rebuffed. Néstor didn't know that his own informants had told him that Jack would soon be unemployed, so if he could get that man to work for him he would really have his finger on the pulse. Perhaps Jack would sell out to him. If not, maybe he could play a part in the future development that looked like being a real goldmine. If not, why would Néstor consider neglecting his lucrative work in Alicante?

There was something in this whole business and Martínez wasn't going to be left out.

6

Sure enough, Jack's parcel of books was waiting for him at the post office and after a short chat with Carmen he walked out into the bright sunshine and strapped the parcel onto his pannier rack. He kicked himself for not mentioning his new role to her, but the news of the arrival of her first granddaughter had made it difficult to get a word in edgeways. He would buy some stamps another day and bring up the subject then.

He rolled his bike down the street and around the corner to the bar with no name. Mario's bar was very much the poor relation of Julio's bar, but its shabby interior and inferior selection of tapas didn't stop the village men from going there, not least because it was cheaper. In these hard times ten or twenty cents saved on a beer or a glass of wine made a difference, especially to those who spent a lot of time there. The village women, on the other hand, if they went to a bar at all, usually went to Julio's and made themselves comfortable at the tables in his tastefully decorated dining room. The British residents, almost without exception, frequented Pam's bar.

This morning there were only two customers in Mario's bar, young men who Jack didn't know. Still, they were sat up at the bar and would hear the conversation that he was determined to have with the owner.

"*Buenos días*, Mario."

"Hola, Jack. What can I get you?"

Mario wasn't a great conversationalist and normally expected his customers to make their own fun, though they could always fall back on the ubiquitous television if they had no-one to talk to.

"A *tostada* with oil and salt, and a coffee, please."

Jack would have preferred to have breakfasted at Julio's, but thought that a piece of toast would buy him time to pluck up the courage to say what he had to say. Mario was a heavy-set man of about his own age, but a life spent mostly perched on a bar stool – his wife, Luisa, did the cooking and cleaning – made him look considerably older and redder. He suffered from gout and was always happy to talk about it.

"How are your feet, Mario?" Jack asked after pouring oil onto his toast.

"Not so bad today. The doctor has ordered me to avoid seafood and alcohol for a month. That was six days ago, so only twenty-four to go," he said, puffing out his cheeks and exhaling disconsolately.

"If it lessens your gout perhaps you should continue to abstain."

"We'll see, but life is dull without a little glass of wine and a couple of shrimps from time to time."

"That's true," said Jack. "Perhaps moderation is the key, and a little exercise."

"Exercise? When I'm stuck in here from morning till night?"

The image of Mario puffing away on a static bicycle in the little used dining room crossed Jack's mind and a flicker of amusement must have played upon his lips.

"What's so funny?" Mario said gruffly.

"What? Oh, I'm just thinking about my new venture," he said, determined to start making inroads into his ten person target. Besides, he had given Mario so much advice on healthy living over the years – all of it ignored – that it was pointless to persist. "I'm no longer working for Brian. Now I intend to act as an intermediary between people who wish to sell property and those who may wish to buy it." He felt the blood rising to his face, but thought that the job description he had decided on that morning had not sounded too bad.

"And get rich, eh?"

"Not at all. I intend to charge the seller a fixed fee for my services. One thousand euros," he said boldly.

Mario raised his eyebrows.

"Unless the property is very small, in which case I'll charge less," he found himself saying.

"No, no, one thousand euros seems very reasonable. I know of cases where the agent, for want of a better word, has made five million pesetas on a seventeen million peseta sale."

"A long time ago, no?"

"Not at all, it's just that I still think in pesetas when larger sums are involved. In the case in question the buyer said to the agent, a fat little fiend from Orihuela, 'Get me twelve million for it'. This he did, but he obtained another five million for himself."

Jack made a quick calculation. "That's about thirty thousand euros! Were the buyers English?"

"Of course; that's to say they were foreigners, probably English. A Spaniard would have realised what was going on in the notary's office, I'm sure."

"What would have gone on there?"

"Well, after the official paperwork had been signed and the official money handed over, the notary would have excused himself for a few minutes. That is when the *dinero negro* is paid. Surely you know that, Jack?"

"Yes, I know it happens, but for the agent to keep all the black money, that's terrible. I've no intention of doing anything like that. I just want a fair commission for… connecting people."

"Ha, that's what they all say at first." Mario waved down the hands that Jack had raised in protest. "No, I know that you aren't that kind of man."

"Thanks."

The two young men left the bar and Jack saw them climb into a delivery van, so they wouldn't have counted even if they had stayed.

"So, Mario, will you mention me to anybody who you think might have a house to sell?"

"No."

"No?"

"No, for two reasons. Firstly, because, as you know, I am not a gossip and if I *think* they have a house to sell, well, it's their business to speak up about it. Secondly, because Marco the baker comes in every day and, as you also know, he has set up his daughter Marta in an estate agent's office not a hundred metres from here."

"I understand," said Jack, not unduly concerned by this inauspicious start to his campaign. "The cooler weather is a relief, I must say."

"Pah! Some go-getting impresario you are, I must say." Mario took Jack's empty plate away and slid it into a sinkful of grimy water.

"What do you mean?"

"That's no way to hustle for business, is it? 'I understand,' he says. Ha, you'll get nowhere like that.

"But if you're friends with Marco, I understand-"

"There you go, understanding again. Persuade me!"

"And how can I do that?"

"Good heavens, Jack. You're as old as me, but you're like a boy sometimes. Why are you embarking on this scheme?"

"Well, to make money."

"And what is it that makes the world go round?"

"Er, money?"

"Right." Mario plucked the plate from the sink, gave it a perfunctory wipe, and dropped it with a clatter onto the clean pile.

"So… what you mean is that you ought to get a… commission too?"

"Oh, I wouldn't call it anything so formal as a commission, but if you sell a house that I told you about and make a thousand euros, it would be a friendly gesture to make me a gift of, say, a hundred."

"Of course, I'd be happy to do that." Jack smiled in an attempt to conceal a worrying thought. With this arrangement if he sold a house that half the village had told him about he might end up in debt.

"I know what you're thinking, Jack," said the veteran of a many a bar counter intrigue. "Obviously if I tell you something that's common knowledge I don't expect to be… recompensed. The thing is there are many people in and around the village who *might* have a house or some land to sell. The trouble is that they don't want anybody to know about it."

"How will they sell it then?"

"They won't, unless the transaction can be made very quietly and the sale price remains undisclosed."

"Pour me a small glass of white wine, please. Why the secrecy? What does it matter?"

Mario served the wine and smiled at Jack. "I thought you knew the people here well enough to know that. What are the people here like?"

"Er, well, they're kind, friendly…"

"Yes, a number of them are both those things. What else? In relation to what we are speaking about, I mean."

Jack sipped the wine and saw the light. "Proud. They are proud."

"Eureka! They are very proud, and the less people have, the prouder they are. So, if somebody who has plenty of money has a wonderful house to sell, he will tell the whole world. 'I am selling this, but just wait until you see what I buy next,' is the message he will give. A person who has to sell property due to financial necessity, on the other hand, feels ashamed, especially now that prices are so low."

Jack nodded, frowned, sipped his wine, and wondered if he should ask Mario if he knew of anybody who might want to learn English.

"That old house down there, for example," Mario went on, pointing towards the end of the street. "Young... well, the man who wants to sell it hasn't worked for some time. His wife does a little cleaning work in the village, but they have two small children and his unemployment benefit is about to run out. He will get no more than €20,000 for the place, probably less, but he will have to sell. Seven or eight years ago I remember him sitting where you are now and telling me that he was about to restore the house in which he was born and sell it to the English, who at that time were swarming about the place looking at property. Then the crash, and nothing. Now he sits on that stool only once or twice a week and never mentions the house, but he will sell it, quietly."

"That's awful. If I helped him to sell the house I wouldn't take a cent."

"Hmm, I'm not sure, but I think Marta is taking care of it. Being Marco's daughter, she won't be as generous as you would."

"She seems like a nice girl."

"She is, but Marco is in charge there."

"So, are many people in a similar position in the village? If that's the case, I think I'll give up the whole idea."

"The example I've given you is the most extreme case I know of. There are other people who want to sell, but their needs are not so pressing."

"Still, it's not what I thought it would be like at all," said Jack. "I'm having my doubts now."

Mario walked around the bar to the door, looked up and down the street, and returned to his stool. "Listen, I'll speak to people who I think might want to sell when I'm alone with them and I'll ask them if they'd like you to look around for a buyer. All this must be done with great discretion," he said, tapping the side of his nose.

"Of course. I appreciate this, Mario."

"And there is one condition."

"What's that?"

"That you spend more time in here than in that scoundrel Julio's bar."

"Ha, I'll do that." He left three coins on the counter. "I'll see you soon."

"I hope so."

Jack had intended to visit the scoundrel Julio after leaving Mario's, but instead decided to go to the little park. He wheeled his bike there, found a bench in the shade, and sat down to think. Merely telling folk about his new venture promised to be a lengthy and draining process and he dismissed the idea of speaking to ten people in one day. His conversation with the unusually loquacious Mario had already given him food for thought.

Prices were so low now that the poor man Mario had mentioned would end up practically giving away what was once his family home. It sounded like others were also being forced to sell and he knew that if he helped them he might end up not charging them a penny. Even in the school playground he had been useless at bartering and he hadn't improved with age. Could he charge the house buyer instead? No, he didn't think that was done.

He was still summoning up the energy to go to Julio's bar – perhaps Mario had been overly pessimistic – when he saw Brian's van coming up the road into the village. A miserable-looking Josh was in the passenger seat and saw Jack on the bench. Jack raised his hand in greeting, but the van had passed before either of them could respond. He felt a pang for his lost livelihood, but tried to see it from Brian's point of view. He had hardly ever had enough work for three people and Josh hadn't done well enough at school to warrant staying on for two more years. Jack just wished he'd been given a little warning.

Yes, now it was time for him to start using his brain rather than his body and with this in mind he stood up, stretched his back, and began to wheel his bike towards Julio's. Just as he reached the main street he heard his name and turned to see Brian walking towards him through the grassless park. Jack saw that the big man look worried and he hoped he hadn't had any bad news.

"Jack, I was hoping to catch you. Are you busy?"

"No, not exactly. Is something the matter?"

"No, well, I just thought I owed you an explanation."

"Don't worry about it, Brian. I understand that family comes first," Jack said, patting his friend on the arm.

"It's not just that. Look, let's go to the bar. I'll be able to explain things better after I've had a beer."

Jack nodded and wheeled his bike onto the pavement and to the right.

"No, not Pam's bar," said Brian. "Let's go to Julio's, it'll be quieter."

Julio's bar was very busy, it now being pre-lunch aperitif time, but seemed to be empty of English speakers, which was Brian's main concern. He pointed to a small table in the corner and asked Jack what he wanted to drink. A few moments later he brought over Jack's glass of white wine and a half-litre glass of beer for himself, glasses which Julio had been quick to stock up on when he saw the foreigners' preference for what they called 'pints'. Shame they almost all went to the Englishwoman's bar now.

Jack noticed that Brian's clothes – sturdy trousers and a sort of fisherman's gilet over his t-shirt – were too clean for him to have done much work that morning. Perhaps he had gone to see about a job. When he took his first sip of wine the so far silent Brian had drunk over half of his beer.

"What's on your mind, Brian?" Jack asked, smiling in what he hoped was an encouraging way.

"I've got something I want to get off my chest, Jack," he said before finishing the beer. "Another wine?"

"Go on then," he said, wishing to put Brian at his ease. Nobody likes to drink alone, after all.

"Right," Brian said as he put down the drinks and took his seat. "Do you know Les? Les and Denise?"

"Yes, I had a brief chat with them one day at Pam's. They live in a new house up past the cemetery, don't they?"

"Yes."

"I remember. He told me he'd sold his haulage firm and was going to live the good life here." Jack recalled the fat, blustery midlander and his large, smiling wife; people whose society he instantly knew he would not be cultivating.

"Well, Les has suddenly decided that he doesn't want to retire after all. He wants to buy property and build houses."

"Hmm, good luck to him. I wouldn't have thought it was a good time to build right now."

"No, nor do I, but I think he's doing it more for fun than anything else. He's already bored."

Par for the course, Jack thought. He had been surprised by how many of the British settlers appeared to have no hobbies or interests. Building work, paperwork and buying things occupy them for the first year or two, and then what? Judging by the conversations he had heard at Pam's bar, not much, but perhaps that was unfair. The ones he didn't see were probably too busy to while away mornings on Pam's makeshift pavement terrace. Jack saw that Brian's glass was empty and stood up.

"Another one?" he asked, knowing that the third pint was often the great tongue loosener.

"Go on then."

When Jack returned with the drinks Brian was sitting up very straight. As soon as Jack made contact with his chair he started to speak.

"Les must have driven round the whole area looking at land. He's decided that he wants to buy your house and all Pedro's land. He wants to build a house for himself on your land and several posh houses on Pedro's land."

Jack finished his second glass of wine and nodded.

"He knows you've no intention of selling, so he wants me to give you no more work, to freeze you out. He plans to buy that old house down past Mario's bar and have me and Josh do it up. After that he hopes to have bought some of Pedro's land and he wants me to start building houses there."

"He could make your fortune," Jack said in a neutral voice.

"He's a bastard. I said I wanted you involved – on the old house and the new project – but he refused. The trouble is he's got to Liz through Denise. You know how keen Liz is to get on."

"Yes." Jack thought about Brian's wife. He'd only ever seen her looking euphorically happy or down in the dumps. He suspected that she wasn't the most stable person in the world and understood that Brian had to tread carefully. It wasn't an easy situation and as Brian was clearly expecting a response Jack decided to go to the toilet to think about it.

When he left the bathroom he saw that Brian had finished half of his third pint, so he quickly ordered three tapas that he knew his friend liked.

"Do you want my opinion on all that you've told me?" Jack asked.

"Of course."

"Well, I think that Les's whole scheme is preposterous. Houses just aren't selling at the moment. Look at all the new builds that are standing empty. Look at the *urbanización* down near Fortuna and the one near Jumilla. Houses with pools there are going for less than half what they expected to sell them for. There are thousands of chalets to sell in Spain before it's worth thinking about building any more."

"They say things are picking up a bit," said Brian with a shrug.

"They'll have to pick up a whole lot more to warrant building luxury houses on Pedro Poveda's land. I like the countryside here, but, if we're honest about it, it's nothing special. It's a good way from the sea and there's a chilly wind up here in winter."

"Les likes to say that what goes down comes up," said Brian, stabbing a piece of fried cheese that Julio had brought over along with a dish of pork in sauce, a plate of cured ham and a small basket of bread.

"Les sounds like a fool to me, who knows nothing about Spain's recent history. Listen, they reckon that the whole housing boom started because of the changeover to the euro in 2002. People had so much money stashed away – *dinero negro* – that from about the year 2000 onwards they started spending it on property, among other things. Then the banks made it easier and easier to borrow – like in Britain, only more so – so even more people started buying. Add the fact that the Spanish economy was doing pretty well during those years and you have a recipe for disaster. Who's been building houses since 2008?"

"Nobody I know," said Brian, who Jack was pleased to see was now eating more than he was drinking. He didn't want him to get home drunk, especially not today.

"Things will pick up slowly, I'm sure, until they reach some kind of normality, but don't expect to see another boom like that one in our lifetimes. Perhaps you should explain all this to Liz."

"Yes, I'll have to choose the right moment."

"And don't say it was me who said it."

"Ha, no."

"You *could* tell her one thing that I've said; that there's absolutely no way that I'm going to sell my house to Les."

"Not even if he offers you a lot more than it's worth?"

"Not for all the tea in China. Tell Liz both those things, separately, and see if she starts seeing sense."

Brian nodded and put down his fork. "She's a bit hyper at the moment, so I might have to wait a bit. In the meantime Les will probably buy that old house. Whether Liz sees the light or not I'm still going to have to accept that job. I've got sod all else on at the moment."

Jack rolled a slice of ham around his fork and placed it between two small slices of bread. He ate, took a sip of wine, and wiped his mouth with his paper napkin. His time spent with Mario earlier in the morning, added to wine he had drunk, seemed to have given him a taste for intrigue.

"On second thoughts, don't tell Les that I won't sell him the house. If he asks you, give him hope. That's what I'll do if he calls me. By doing that, he'll be more likely to buy the old house and that'll keep you and Josh in work until something else comes up."

"It's an idea, but I still feel bad about you not being able to work on it with me."

"Don't worry about me. I've got a few ideas and I think it's about time I stopped doing building work anyway. My back's not up to the heavy stuff anymore. Once you've made a start on the house and Les comes back to pester me some more about buying mine I'll take great delight in telling him to piss off." Jack giggled and pushed his wineglass away. "Four glasses in the morning is too much for me. No, I'll keep him hanging on till you're well into that job to make sure he doesn't get cold feet. That's if he buys the house and it's not all talk."

"Oh, he'll buy it all right. Liz told me that Denise told her that he's offered the bloke fifteen thousand and that he's thinking about it."

"Fifteen thousand!" Jack slapped his hand down on the table. "That's robbery! That's exploiting a man who's out of work and has two kids to feed."

"Yes, he asked twenty and I don't know why Les couldn't just have paid it. Part of his fun, I suppose, but he'll make no friends round here behaving like that."

"People like him couldn't care less about what people think. I wish he'd bought a house somewhere else, like Italy."

"Yes, perhaps that would've been best. I'd better get home for lunch now, Jack. I'll get this."

"Thanks, Brian. Anyway, we'll keep in touch and see how things pan out."

"Yes." Brian looked slightly less worried than he had done an hour earlier. "Thanks for all the advice."

"Thank *you* for telling me what's going on."

7

After Brian had left the bar Jack's only desire was to leave the village, that Babylon of intrigue, and return to the refuge of his home. He pedalled along the main street, freewheeled down the half mile of road, and laboured up the track to his house, pushing harder than usual and breaking into a sweat before he reached the open gate. Keen to dispel the effects of the wine, he took his hoe from the porch and weeded vigorously for half an hour, before picking some tomatoes and returning to the house. After a long drink of water and a quick shower he ate a cheese, tomato and lettuce sandwich and made a pot of coffee.

He took a cup of coffee and a box file containing most of his paperwork to the porch table and strove to ascertain if the idea that he had been turning over in his mind was viable. Seeing that it was, at least in theory, he resolved to push the audacious plan to the back of his mind for the time being. Life had been so peaceful and enjoyable until a couple of weeks ago and he had to remind himself that no matter how irksome his current troubles were, he was still much better off than most people. His wide reading, an activity he had begun towards the end of his years in Murcia, helped him in this respect.

Now he had to make a choice. He could withdraw into his shell and ignore the events that were about to unfold. He could bide his time, spend as little money as possible, and wait for the confounded Les to abandon his stupid venture. As for house selling, why get into something that didn't suit him at all? Yes, a few months spent reading, pottering on the land, walking, seeing Vicente and Salvador occasionally; that might be just the thing. He could get some chickens, something he had always put off due to noise they make. There was really no need to go into the village more than once a week and if he stayed away from the bars people would soon get the message; annoy Jack and he disappears. He had read a book about hermits and there was a lot to be said for that way of life. Perhaps Vicente was right and he should sell the car that was already gathering dust again. He could probably live on as little as three or four hundred euros a month which would be good practice for the future.

Jack laughed and drained his coffee cup. "Yes, and I could grow a huge beard too; that would save on razors," he said aloud. The recollection of the man who was about to practically give away his patrimony to Les crossed his mind and he went to pour himself another cup. He must know the man, by sight at least, and it struck him that this was the first time that the presence of foreigners was going to be detrimental to the villagers. Les would be despised, and wouldn't care, but the so far harmonious, almost symbiotic, coexistence might be endangered. He, Jack Birtwell, was the only person, as far as he knew, who could do anything about it.

His reverie was interrupted by the sound of a tractor in the distance. He shaded his eyes and saw old Pedro ploughing between the olive trees down in the valley. He knew it was Pedro by the way he hunched himself over the wheel, but at four o'clock it could hardly be anybody else. His son would still be in the bar, maybe hearing about the fat *inglés* who was about to buy up the property of all the people who were struggling. News travelled fast in the village and became embellished as it did so. Jack tightened his sandals and set off down the track.

"*Buenas tardes*, Pedro," Jack said as the tractor shuddered to a halt at the end of the row where he was waiting.

"*Buenas*, Jack," the old man said before stepping gingerly to the ground. As they shook hands Jack was pleased to feel that Pedro's grip was as strong as ever.

"I saw you and just thought I'd pop down for a chat. How are things with you?"

"Well. Apart from the rheumatism, I'm doing fine."

Jack looked at the rows ploughed and those still to plough and couldn't see much difference.

"The more one ploughs, the better things grow, and it will rain soon," said Pedro, laughing hoarsely. "Did you want to speak to me about anything in particular, Jack?"

"No, I just saw you and thought I'd come and have a chat."

"You've said that once. Is young Puig bothering you too?"

"Puig? Néstor Puig? I've never met him."

"He came down here yesterday, getting dust on his pretty shoes. He asked me if I wanted to sell the land."

"What did you tell him?"

"The same as I told him last week – nothing. I drove away, but the persistent little devil was waiting for me at the end of the next row. He said he only wanted one field, the one bordering your land, and I said no."

"I'm glad. Do you know that he wants to build great big houses with swimming pools?"

"I guessed as much. He also asked me about your house and land."

"What did he ask?"

"If I thought you'd sell." He took a cigarette from the packet in his shirt pocket and lit it. "He spoke about you as if you were some kind of intruder. He's the damn intruder. I told him you weren't planning on going anywhere, as far as I knew."

"Thanks. He's working on behalf of an Englishman who wants to turn the whole area into a development."

"I thought all that silly business had finished a few years ago."

"Me too. Still, if neither of us is going to sell he'll have to take his silly schemes elsewhere."

Pedro took a long pull on his cigarette and looked over the fields towards Jack's house. "I'm not so sure about that, Jack. I'm getting old now, you know."

"But you wouldn't sell, to him, would you?"

"I don't want to, but I sometimes think that if I don't start sorting things out before I die my children will be at each other's throats. Only Pedrito is still here. He's almost sixty now and has never been as keen on the land as me. The other three are living in Madrid and Valencia, so when I go they might start squabbling. I might get it divided up into four parts and make them draw lots. Then they can do what they want with it. I'll hold Pedrito's part back so that I'll have something to do while I'm still around. You don't like the sound of that, do you?"

"I just never thought you'd sell, but I see your point. It would be such a shame if they started building on this land, especially when there are so many houses standing empty."

"Well, don't worry too much for now. I sent young Puig packing, but I expect he'll be back to annoy me again soon."

"Will you let me know if you decide to sell?"

"Of course I will. It'll all take time, in any case."

Not much time, if Les and Néstor get their act together, Jack thought as he plodded disconsolately back across the fields. On entering the house he opened the parcel of books and put them on the 'to read' shelf of the third pine bookcase he had made since moving in. He had always liked to imagine himself surrounded by books in his old age and realised that the belt-tightening that might soon be necessary would put paid to his monthly parcel from England. He ordered his books by letter from a large second-hand bookseller in Rossendale who was forever trying to persuade him to place his orders online. He sometimes spent as much as €100 a month on books and didn't consider it a luxury. Well, he would just have to reread some of the old ones. Why did he keep them, after all?

He made a cup of tea before picking up the Thesiger book, *Arabian Sands*, and settling down in one of his two easy chairs. The book was about the upper class adventurer's travels across the Empty Quarter of Arabia with the nomadic tribes in the 1940s and Jack was amused and impressed by the writer's nonchalance in the face of danger. Right from the start it was clear that Thesiger lamented the changes that were taking place to the Bedouin way of life that had remained the same for hundreds, if not thousands, of years.

'Change and decay in all around I see,' sprang to Jack's mind when he moved out onto the porch to enjoy the afternoon breeze. The world had changed so much in the last two centuries and Jack couldn't understand why people didn't worry more about the way things were heading. 'How many more people can the earth support?' he had once asked Salvador, his cleverest friend, who had replied that it wasn't worth worrying about. Jack did worry though and, rather selfishly it sometimes seemed to him, had chosen to live the rest of his life in a place where he hoped the changes would be less apparent.

He closed the book and looked down the valley. An expanse of cultivated fields stretching away to the hills with only a few old *fincas* dotted around. After the housing crash he had thought that this view would remain unaltered in his lifetime, but now he wasn't so sure. He reviewed the events of the last couple of days and examined the position of the main players. Les had a whim which fuelled Néstor and Martínez's desire to make money; that was the long and short of it. Remove that whim, or channel it elsewhere, and the problem would be solved. Or was it so simple?

If old Pedro was going to sell anyway, the absurd seed that Les had planted might make other people wish to build on the land in the valley, even if Les gave up on the idea when he realised that his main target, Jack's house, was not for sale. He got the impression that Les and Denise were quite sociable, so if they were going around extolling the virtues of the area, other well-heeled foreigners might want a piece of the action too. The thing was to nip the whole affair in the bud.

Les's strategy started with the purchase of the old house in the village. Get Brian on board and fire him with ambition through his loopy wife, leave Jack workless and force him to sell the house that he coveted, and take it from there. Néstor and Martínez would see that he didn't lose enthusiasm if he ever got that far. The result? More unsold chalets and – the only consolation – Les's probable bankruptcy. Jack reopened his book, but could no longer concentrate on the traveller's account. He brought his mobile phone from the house and rang Mario.

"Sí."

"Mario, it's Jack."

"Sí."

"I wanted to ask you something."

"Ask me."

"The man who might be selling the old house at the end of your street. Where does he live?"

"Why?"

"Because I want to speak to him."

"Why?"

"Because, well, I want to see what position he's in regarding the house. I might be able to help him."

"How?"

"Well, never mind that now, but I've heard that this Les has offered him fifteen thousand and that he might accept."

"What? Fifteen thousand? That's… that's criminal."

"I know."

"And the man in question, well, he'll spend that money in a year and will then have nothing. It'll be good for my business, but not for his family," said Mario, overcoming his avowed aversion to telephones. "When he has money, you see, like he used to have when he was driving the digger, he spends it."

"Does he drink a lot or something?"

"He drinks, but his main problem is the machines."

"Diggers?"

"No, slot machines. My earnings from the *tragaperras* will rise, but I don't like to make money in that way."

"No," said Jack before pausing for thought. "So, whatever he got for the house, he'd waste it anyway?"

"Well, there's always that danger, but with such a small sum he may say, 'To hell with it,' and waste the money. The humiliation, you see."

"Hmm. I'd like to speak to him in any case."

"He lives on the row of newer houses behind the supermarket. The first one if you approach from Marco's bakery."

"Right. What's his name?"

"Jose Miguel, or Josemi."

"Thanks, Mario."

"Come and see me soon."

"I will."

Jack went inside to fetch his box file. After re-examining the pertinent papers he was about to ring Salvador when the phone rang in his hand.

"Hello?"

"Jack, it's Les here. We met once at Pam's bar, me and the wife."

"Ah, yes, I remember. What can I do for you, Les?"

"Well, I wanted to ask you... if it's not a bit forward, I was wondering if you'd ever considered selling your house."

What a good actor he is, Jack thought. So polite, so diffident. "Er, well, it's not something I've ever thought about. I'm not really planning on moving, you see."

"No, well, anyway, I'd just like to say that if you ever considered it, I'd be prepared to give you €125,000 for it."

"Hmm, that's a fair price, the way things are at the moment, but, as I say, I'm not thinking about selling. My work's here, with Brian, you see."

"Brian?"

"Yes, he's a builder."

"Oh, yes, I've met him and his wife Liz," said Les.

"Things are a bit quiet at the moment, but I've been working for him for years and I'm sure things will soon pick up."

"Yes, they always do. Anyway, sorry to have bothered you, but if you reconsider, just let me know."

"I will."

"I'm looking at other places too, so... anyway, nice to talk to you."

"You too, Les. See you later."

Jack smiled, feeling that he had given Les enough hope to prevent him from carrying out his plans with undue haste. His desire to speak to Salvador, however, was undiminished, so he found his number and pressed the green button.

"Hola."

"Salva, it's Jack. A quick question."

"Good afternoon to you too, Jack."

"Ha, listen, if one wanted to buy a house, how quickly could the paperwork be done?"

"Who's buying a house?"

"Nobody, it's just something I need to know."

"Well, if a standard survey is all that's required and the lawyer works fast, the contract can be drawn up quite quickly. You're not selling, are you?"

"No, no, it's just something I needed to know."

There was a pause on the other end of the line. "Don't do anything without consulting me, Jack?"

"I wouldn't dream of it. Do you fancy lunch here on Saturday?"

"I fear that Chelo requires my company at her mother's house. I could manage *almuerzo*."

"Great. I'll expect you around ten. Don't bring anything."

"I'm intrigued."

"There's probably nothing to be intrigued about. See you then."

Jack hung up the phone for the third time, dropped it onto the table, and sighed. He opened his book and tried to immerse himself in another, more tranquil world.

8

Jack's phone didn't ring again that day, but on the following day, a Thursday, as he was cycling along under a heavy sky, its insistent tones obliged him to roll to a halt just short of the village.

"Hola, is that Jack?"

"Sí."

"*Qué tal*, Jack? It's Martínez here."

"Martínez? Which Martínez?"

"The builder, Adán Martínez, from the village," he said. He spoke like a gruff, impatient man making an effort to sound pleasant.

"What can I do for you, Adán?"

"Could we meet, Jack? I'd like to speak to you about, well, something I want to discuss."

"Sounds interesting. I'm busy this morning, but..." Jack reconsidered and decided that it would be better to hear what this man had to say before seeking out the owner of the old house. "No, on second thoughts, this morning would be fine."

"Can we meet at Julio's bar in half an hour?"

"Sooner would be better. I've got a lot of things to do today."

"In ten minutes then."

To kill time – he didn't want the third degree from Julio before he met the builder – he located Josemi's home on a row of modern, two-storey houses with large patios to the rear. These houses, built by Martínez eight or nine years earlier, had been much sought after by the villagers, but their poor quality was beginning to show; long cracks in the walls and signs of damp still evident so long after the spring rains. Jack sighed and headed to the bar to meet their creator.

Martínez looked like a man who lived on his nerves and probably got on the nerves of the people who worked for him, Jack thought as he approached him at the bar. At half past nine there was nobody else at the bar counter, but Martínez, after smiling grimly and shaking hands, led Jack to a table in the far corner. When Julio brought their coffees he smiled at Jack and raised his eyebrows slightly, presumably in encouragement. With the image of the cracked walls still in mind he wondered if Julio and Martínez were related in any way. They had the same eyes and maybe if you packed forty pounds of fat around the builder's wiry frame the resemblance would be greater. Jack stirred his *cortado* and waited.

"Well, er, Jack, what I wanted to speak to you about was work," said Martínez, the strain of smiling exacerbating his premature wrinkles. He wasn't yet forty, but Jack supposed that a life of hustling for jobs and doing them shoddily wasn't a recipe for tranquillity of countenance.

"What about work?" he asked, showing Martínez what a real smile looked like.

"I've got a lot of work on at the moment, mainly in other villages, and I wondered if you'd be interested in doing some work for me."

"I work for Brian, the English builder."

"Ah, Brian, yes, I know him, not well, because my English is very poor. Is he... busy?"

"Not at the moment, but something will come up soon, I'm sure. I only work two or three days a week and I often take breaks. I'm sixty now, you see, and like to take it easy."

"Yes, I see." Martínez nodded very quickly several times and bared his white teeth in an especially forced grimace. "Nevertheless, if you find that things become... very slow, you know that I have work for you. I pay my skilled workers high rates."

"Oh, I'm not skilled, Adán. I'm little more than a labourer really."

"I also pay my labourers very well."

"The trouble is that my back isn't as strong as it used to be. I've been having some problems lately."

"Oh, but you wouldn't be required to do the really heavy work. I have youngsters to do that, ha ha."

"But a labourer who doesn't do heavy work? That's unusual."

"Yes, but there are always little jobs... essential jobs, but not so heavy."

Jack considered asking if he could just make the tea, or rather coffee, but Martínez's face had become so contorted with false bonhomie that Jack decided to give him a break. "Listen, I'll bear in mind what you've said and if I need work I'll give you a call."

"Good." His face relaxed into a frown. "Here's my card."

"Thanks." He examined the bilingual card. "How did you get my number, by the way?"

"Oh, I asked Julio. I... I always come in here. I hope to hear from you soon."

"You might, Adán. Thanks for the coffee."

Jack bought a long baguette from Marco's assistant at the bakery and strapped it to the pannier rack before heading back to the street of cracked houses. He thought he had set the right tone with Martínez and hoped that his conversation with Josemi would go as smoothly. A slim, pretty woman answered the door and her enquiring look turned into a frown when he asked if her husband was at home.

"Why do you wish to see him?" she asked.

"Oh, I just wanted to ask him about the old house that I've heard he's selling."

Jack's reason for calling, and his benign smile, erased the anxious expression from the young woman's face. Maybe his gambling has got them into debt, Jack surmised as he was shown into a neat dining room. She returned with her husband, a man of forty whose muscular frame was padded out with too much fat, and after introductions were made – she was called Esperanza – the three of them sat down around the large round table. Josemi, who Jack had seen once or twice before, seemed annoyed that his wife had elected to stay, but she had no intention of missing what this foreigner had to say.

"I wanted to ask you about the house that I believe is for sale on Calle de la Cruz," Jack said to Josemi, but also looking at his wife.

"Yes, it is for sale," Josemi said, feigning indifference.

"How much are you asking for it?"

"Thirty thousand euros."

Jack saw a flicker of surprise pass over the woman's stern face and realised the delicacy of the situation. He could hardly say, 'Look pal, I know you've been offered fifteen thousand and will probably take it, so let's be realistic.' He nodded slowly while trying to decide what to say next.

"Er, well, that's a little more than I'm able to pay," was the best he could come up with.

"That's the price," said Josemi, drawing a rapid glance of barely perceptible annoyance from his wife.

Jack realised that he would have to be bolder. "It's just that I'd heard a foreigner called Les had made you an offer. You know how news travels in the village." He laughed apologetically, but neither of them appeared to share his amusement. Oh well, bolder still. "Listen, I've heard that the *inglés* has offered you fifteen thousand and that you are considering the offer. That is shameful and scandalous and I'm prepared to pay you twenty-two thousand for the house, on one condition."

"What condition?" they asked almost simultaneously.

"That I pay you half of the money now and half in one year's time. This will be stipulated in the contract," he went on quickly to stem any protests, "which, if you agree, will be drawn up by the lawyer Salvador Torrente. Don't worry, I'm perfectly solvent, but I'll need time to release some of the money from my English investment accounts," he lied, as all his savings were in one of the few Spanish banks to have weathered the economic crisis unscathed.

Josemi drummed his fingers on the table and did not meet his wife's questioning look.

"I can only pay two thousand in black money," Jack decided to add. "So that would be twelve on concluding the sale and ten exactly one year after that. Salvador is a very well-respected and trustworthy lawyer and I am also a man of my word, so there is no danger of me delaying the final payment," he said. Speaking like this felt very odd, but it seemed like the best way to proceed.

"We know Salvador and I also know that you have lived here for a long time," said Esperanza, glancing at Josemi.

Jack suspected that she knew the real reason for his dual payment proposal and saw its advantages. If her husband blew the first instalment she would be able to keep a tighter rein on the second. Jack hoped that two years would be long enough for the man to find work, and if not, well, he would have tried his best.

"I'd like to have a good look at the house first, of course," he said.

"What will you do with it?" asked Josemi, raising his liquid brown eyes from the table.

"I will restore it. Some relatives in England are hoping to move here and the house will probably be for them." Two lies in as many minutes was unprecedented for Jack, but he assured himself that they were white ones.

"But you wouldn't be able to sell it until you had made both payments," said Esperanza.

"Of course not. The contract would make that impossible."

"I'll show you the house," said Josemi, standing quickly and leaving the room.

"What do you think, Esperanza?" Jack asked in a low voice.

"I like the arrangement and will try to convince him," she whispered. "He had high hopes for the house at one time, but now... now the sale will be a great help to us."

Josemi stood in the doorway with a bunch of keys in his hand and Jack followed him out of the house. He frowned when he saw Jack's bike leaning against the wall and led the way down the street. Jack decided to take his bike along as he thought Josemi would prefer to walk back alone. Here was a wounded man, but he hardly expected him to kiss his hand for delivering him from the complete humiliation of selling for an even lower price to the rich, fat *inglés*.

As they walked along in silence Jack hoped that his much deliberated plan would not receive a setback when the interior of the house was revealed. He had seen that the roof appeared basically sound and was confident that he could restore the property and make a reasonable profit on its sale a couple of years hence. Maybe even a handsome profit if he waited for things to really pick up. His initial thought had been to offer €25,000, but he wasn't a sister of mercy and had to act shrewdly. The project would keep him busy for a while and it would be satisfying to put into practice all that Brian had taught him over the years. He would nip Les's war of attrition in the bud and make him see that he was not to be trifled with. Brian and his son would miss out on the work, but if you throw your lot in with a man like Les you can't expect too much compassion. The cost of the house and the restoration would make a tremendous dent in his savings, but, all things considered, he didn't think it such a rash move.

"Dragged kicking and screaming into the capitalist class," he muttered to himself.

"What's that?" asked Josemi.

"Oh, just thinking aloud."

Josemi unlocked the door of the off-white, one-storey house in the middle of a row of five similar dwellings and pushed it open. "Take a good look around," he said. "I'll wait for you here."

Happy to leave the moody man outside – there was clearly going to be no sales patter today – Jack made his way through the dusty lobby into the living room. As he walked through all the rooms the anxiety that had hit him on entering the house gradually left him and turned to a feeling of anticipation. The living room, dining room and three bedrooms needed retiling, replastering and painting. The kitchen needed that too, as well as a new set of units. The green bathroom would have to be changed for a white one – easy enough – and the window frame was rotten with damp. Well, a set of new windows had already been factored into his rough calculations. The patio to the rear wouldn't need too much work, unless he decided to replace the terracotta tiles, one or two of which were cracked. The door from the patio to the street was rotten, so that made three doors to change. The internal doors might do if he repainted them, but new ones would be better.

"This house is a Tardis," he murmured as he retraced his steps through all the substantial rooms. From looking at the façade he hadn't imagined that such a large house lay behind it and the sale price began to seem very reasonable, but it was no gift because to renovate it properly would be costly. When he located the hatch to the loft area his anxiety returned and he fetched an old stepladder he had seen in the dining room, pushed open the hatch, and climbed up to take a look. Without a torch he couldn't see much, but what he saw pleased him; concrete beams. So the house wasn't so old, after all. He saw no chinks of light through the roof and smiled with relief. A new roof would have meant getting a real builder in.

He made a final tour of the rooms, switching the lights on and off as he went. The electrics would need inspecting, but he didn't think a full rewire would be necessary. After he had turned all the taps on and off and examined the colour of the water he thought it was time to get back to Josemi.

"It looks all right," he said. "Bigger than I expected."

"It's a fine house," said Josemi, before flicking his cigarette butt across the street.

"Yes, well, I'll leave you to think about my offer. Here's my number." He handed him a slip of paper.

"I would accept your offer now, but for one thing," said Josemi, looking down the street.

"What's that, Josemi?"

"Your insistence on making two payments."

"As I said, my money in England-"

"Pah, that is nonsense," he snapped. "If your bank account were in China you could dispose of the money within a short time if you wished. I know you're a good man, or so they say in the village, and I think the gossips have told you that I'm likely to squander the money." He looked at Jack squarely for the first time.

"Yes, there's some truth in that."

"Listen, the two thousand in black money would be spent immediately in paying off debts – household debts – and the rest would stay in the bank until required. My wife administers the money now."

"Right, no problem."

"So you'll pay the full amount immediately?"

"Yes."

"Then I agree. You can get Salvador to draw up the contract."

He offered Jack his hand, but his face remained solemn while they shook.

"I'll see Salva the day after tomorrow," said Jack. Josemi's brief experiment with eye contact appeared to be over. "You don't seem too pleased about it."

"Jack, you know I would have had to accept the offer of that fat English *cabrón*, so why do you offer so much more? I don't want your charity." Josemi looked hard at Jack, who responded with a warm smile.

"We can make it seventeen thousand if you prefer," he said, still smiling.

"Too late. We have shaken hands," Josemi said. His face softened as Jack's placid gaze calmed him and he couldn't help but smile too.

"It's not charity by any means, Josemi. It's not even a very good price, but nor is it greedy exploitation of a man going through a difficult time. I have very good reasons for buying your house which might prevent me from going through similar difficulties. I may explain this to you one day, but for now I have just one more thing to ask you and I hope you won't interpret it in the wrong way."

"Ask."

"I'm going to restore the house as I can't afford to pay other people to do it, but my back is not so strong and I'll need help with the heavier work. Would you be able to help me one or two days a week? I'll pay you in cash and nobody will comment because we can say it was part of the deal."

Josemi pursed his lips and moved his head from side to side in deliberation. Jack squeezed the muscular bicep of the man's left arm.

"What do you say, Josemi? I can pay you ten euros an hour."

"And will you also tell me how to spend that money?"

"Ha, no, do what you want with it."

"I'll not waste it. I've finished with the *tragaperra* machines for good."

"Good. I'll call you after I've spoken to Salva."

"All right." Josemi looked the house up and down. "The roof is good, you know."

"I know, but there's plenty more to do. How are the plumbing and electrics?"

"Not so old, but they will need checking."

"Younger than me, that's for sure. Ah, there's just one more thing. For now, please don't tell anybody who is buying the house. If Les calls you and makes a better offer, feel free to accept it, but please don't mention my name."

"We've shaken on it, Jack, and I have nothing more to say to that man."

"Good. See you soon."

"See you, Jack, and thanks."

9

Jack was picking peppers and tomatoes when he heard Salva's noisy car begin the ascent of the track. He took his penknife from his pocket, sliced off a lettuce, and carried the basket back to the house. The sky was heavy to the northwest and he knew it was going to rain very soon, so his irrigation system – a series of perforated plastic tubes that covered every tree and furrow – could be left idle for the first time since the end of May. He frowned at the thought of working on the house *and* his land, but reminded himself that there was no hurry to finish the house as property prices could surely only rise from now on. Perhaps if he got a really good price for it he would give Josemi and Esperanza some more money, especially if they were still struggling. Could he do that without offending Josemi? He would find a way if he made a large profit, but that was unlikely.

"You look lost in thought there, Jack," said Salva as he closed the car door.

"Hola, Salva. Yes, I have a lot to think about. How are you?"

"I'm well, and becoming busier at work."

"That's good, and I have a little more for you."

"How's that, Jack?"

"Let's eat first, then I'll explain."

They entered the house and Jack prepared two bacon and egg *bocadillos* – an English 'recipe' which Salva liked a lot, including the HP Sauce that Jack treated himself to when he made one of his rare visits to the English shop in Mónovar, normally after visiting the bank. While the bacon – or rather *panceta*, the rather fatty Spanish equivalent – was cooking, he made a salad and opened a bottle of red wine from the cooperative.

"Let's eat outside and watch the rain clouds gather," he said while he added olive oil, salt and vinegar to the salad.

"What's the news, then?" Salvador asked a few moments later with a mouth full of sandwich.

"If I tell you now you'll choke."

Salvador chewed, sipped his wine, and smiled. "Don't tell me you've bought a house?"

"How did you know?"

"Why else would you ask what you asked on the phone the other day?"

"I'm going to buy an old house on Calle de la Cruz belonging to a young couple called Josemi and Esperanza."

"I know them and I think I know the house."

"The wealthy Englishman, Les, was going to buy it and have Brian and his son do the restoration work, on the condition that I was *not* to be employed. He thought that by taking away my work he'd be able to force me to sell this house to him, which he needs for his stupid housing project. Well, I will soon have *two* houses and plenty of work."

Jack took a bite out of his sandwich while Salva chewed pensively.

"Can you afford it?" he asked.

"Just about. Josemi accepted my offer of twenty-two thousand; seven more than the *cabrón* Les offered him."

"One third more? Have you become a registered charity?"

"The house is easily worth it. It's structurally sound and I'll renovate it myself, with some help from Josemi."

"Is that part of the deal?"

"No, I'll be paying him."

"He'll throw the money into the *tragaperras*."

"He says not, and I believe him. Anyway, that's his business. Listen, Salva, I don't care too much what the other English people around here do, but I won't have Les sullying our name by humiliating a village family. What do you think?"

Salva finished an especially large mouthful, drained his wine glass, and wiped his mouth with a napkin. "I think it's an excellent idea, providing you can afford to live until you sell the house, preferably at least two years from now when the market will have improved. If you are lucky," he said, tapping the top of his head with his fist, "this venture could go some way to solving your financial problems."

"I'm relieved that you think it's a good idea."

"I'd have thought of it first, of course, only I didn't imagine that you'd want to take on so much work."

"Only three or four days a week, and with Josemi to help me with the heavier work, such as removing the old floor tiles. It won't be so much different to working for Brian and it will be a satisfying project. You could even say that it will culminate my building career." He laughed and sipped his wine.

"Yes, because you'll soon be too old for that sort of thing, eh? If you like, I'll call on Josemi and Esperanza this afternoon and on Monday I'll arrange a survey. Next week I'll also visit the town hall in Monóvar and by Friday I'll have drawn up the contract and made an appointment with the notary, so we'll be all set."

"Thanks. I'd like to clinch the sale as quickly as possible in case Les finds out and makes them an offer they can't refuse. Josemi says his word stands, but every man has his price."

"But if this Les is a good businessman, he'll realise that the house is not worth more right now."

"I think he's *been* a successful businessman – he had a fleet of lorries – but this is more of a hobby, even an obsession, and a few thousand either way is nothing to him."

"I'll work quickly and before you know it we'll all be sitting in the notary's office in Monóvar. How much *dinero negro*?"

"Just two thousand."

"That's not much."

"I don't have piles of money under my bed. Besides, to us English that kind of transaction is unusual. We don't like carrying a lot of cash around."

"The Spanish are more daring in their business affairs."

"Yes, and look where it's got them. Coffee?"

"Please. This Les hasn't approached me about any legal work. I wonder which lawyer he's using."

"Néstor. I think he's involved in this scheme of Les."

"That would figure. Crooks like to stick together. They won't be happy when they find out what you've done."

"No. Nor will Brian, because he'll miss out on a large job, and nor will Martínez because he hoped to recruit me to his cause. I won't be very popular with some people."

He went inside to make the coffee and when he emerged with the tray Salvador was deep in thought. He wondered if there was an expression in Spanish for 'a penny for your thoughts' and decided that there wasn't.

"You must insure the house as soon as you buy it, Jack."

"Of course."

"I can arrange that. Is this house insured?"

"Yes. Why the concern?"

"Oh, I don't know, but on you mentioning the name Néstor my thoughts turned to such things."

"I know he's supposed to be a shady character, but surely he's not a criminal?"

"He has the mind of a criminal, that's for sure, but many of my more successful colleagues share that trait. Now I must go home and shave before the delightful family lunch that awaits me," he said, inspecting the gathering clouds.

"It would be best not to mention my... acquisition to anyone until the contract's signed."

"Not a word. What does Vicente think of your entrepreneurial endeavours?"

"He doesn't know yet. He'll probably think I'm mad."

"Ah, these civil servants don't have to face the decisions that we common people have to make in order to get by. A job for life is a fine thing."

"It wouldn't suit you."

"No, I don't suppose it would."

As they cleared the table the rain began to fall and they returned to the shelter of the porch to watch it.

"I love the rain," said Salva, "especially after the long summer."

"I've learnt to appreciate it over the years too."

"Does it rain much in Accrington?"

"More than you could imagine. There's a bag of vegetables for you there."

Salvador stood up and examined the contents. "Fruit of our fertile earth. Thanks." He looked down into the darkening valley. "I wonder if this man Les has thought of making a golf course."

"Ha, please, not even in jest."

Salvador laughed and made a dash for his car.

Before settling down to a quiet afternoon Jack decided to ring Josemi in order to put his mind at ease.

"Josemi? It's Jack. Salva will call on you this afternoon. It seems that the sale can go through quite quickly."

"That's good. I'm feeling happier about it all now. I may use some of the money to buy a delivery van as my cousin in Petrer says he has work for me."

"That's great. What would you be delivering?"

"He imports all kinds of leather good. Bags, belts, shoes – all sorts of things. I'd be self-employed."

"It's a risk. Are you sure the work is there?"

"My cousin assures me it is, and he's trustworthy. I just can't see much digger driving work coming up any time in the next few years."

Jack visualised Les's luxury housing project desecrating the valley. "No, I can't see it either. There are too many houses and flats already built. So perhaps you won't be able to work on the house after all."

"Oh, I will. My cousin wants me to start in November, so the more work you give me before then, the better."

"I think two days a week is the most I can afford, really. I have to keep costs down and do most of it myself. I suppose I'll get somebody else in to install the new windows, as it's a tricky job."

"Nonsense, Jack. I can install windows in my sleep."

"Really?"

"Not literally, of course, but before I got my digger licence I worked as an *albañil* for several years."

"Ah, I didn't know that. So perhaps I'll be doing the labouring work when you are with me."

"Whatever works best. The lawyer Néstor called me this morning on behalf of Les."

Jack felt the blood rush to his face. "Oh, right. What did he say?"

"Ha, it was funny. First he urged me to accept the offer of fifteen thousand. He said Les was looking at another old house and would only give me another few days to decide."

"What did you say?"

"I said that I'd inspected the house more thoroughly and realised that it was in better condition than I'd thought. I told him that if I couldn't get thirty thousand for it I would do it up myself. He asked me to wait a moment. The *inglés* was with him and I heard him speaking, sounding very annoyed, though of course I couldn't understand what he said. Néstor then told me that the *inglés* would pay twenty-five thousand – including ten in cash – if I agreed immediately."

Jack felt a prickling sensation rising from his neck to his head. "Well, that beats me, Josemi."

"Jack, we shook on it, remember? I only asked for thirty thousand out of curiosity. Anyway, I refused and the two of them talked some more, the *inglés* very loudly and Néstor as if he were trying to reason with him. Néstor then said that I drove a very hard bargain, but that he would come round to my house immediately with a pre-contract for the sale; twenty thousand plus ten thousand in cash."

"You should accept, Josemi. It's a lot more money. What did you say?"

"I told him that, on second thoughts, I'd decided that the house was worth forty thousand. He went quiet, but didn't speak to the *inglés*. Then he became annoyed and said that I was acting like a fool. I told him to tell the *inglés* to go and fuck himself and take his stinking money elsewhere. Shame I can't speak English or I would have told him myself."

"Ha, that's funny. Rash, but funny. What did Néstor say to that?"

"He hung up. I may have missed out on some money, but I feel great right now. It's about pride, you see, and I haven't had much of that for the last couple of years."

"I see what you mean, and I appreciate you respecting our agreement. When I see you I'll tell you why it's so important for me to buy your house. Pride is involved there too. I'll see you sometime next week."

"Yes, now I'm going to drink two beers; one at Mario's and one at Julio's. By tomorrow the whole village will know what I've told Néstor and the *inglés*."

"You do that, and thanks again."

Jack switched off his phone – he'd had enough excitement for one day – and made a cup of tea. He chuckled to himself as he sat on the porch watching the rain drilling into the earth. *Orgullo*, pride, that was something that the Spanish took very seriously, and quite rightly. Les's fury would no doubt increase when he found out that he, old Jack, had bought the house. Would Les ever find out how much he had paid? If he didn't he would assume that Jack had paid a lot, thus Jack was solvent, thus Jack would never need to sell his house. Game over.

He switched his phone back on.

"Josemi, it's me again. Listen, could you and Esperanza do me a big favour?"

"If we can, yes."

"Would you mind not telling anyone how much I'm paying for the house? I'll explain why soon, but it would help me with a little problem that I'm having."

"Is that problem called Les?"

"Ha, yes."

"Don't worry. Esperanza and I are just as keen as you are for the sale price to remain a mystery."

"Excellent. Bye for now."

Jack switched off the phone again and walked over to his bookcase. Thesiger's Arabs would have to wait for now, as it was time to delve into his copy of the *Manual Práctico de Construcción*.

10

The next morning Jack sat on the porch enjoying the fresh smells produced by the sunshine after a whole night of rain. He liked the way it rained here; not too often but with a vengeance, far better than the perpetual dampness of Lancashire. That's how he remembered it now, though he could still recall the warm summers of his childhood. Once he was installed in his office job, however, he often missed out on the good days when he could get up onto the moors to walk his dog.

Dogs. He hadn't had one when he was in Murcia, a city being no place for them, but he now missed watching Toby romp around on the land. "Toby was a great cat chaser, you know," he said to the black tomcat that now allowed itself to be stroked. "So you might not like it when I get a new one." He would have to pop into Pam's bar one day and ask her if she knew of any puppies which needed a home, as it was high time that he acquired a new silent, or mostly silent, companion.

He was flicking through the building book when the phone rang. He didn't know the number and considered ignoring it – Sunday was a day of rest, after all – but after seven or eight rings he pressed the green button.

"Hola."

"Hola, Jack. This is Néstor Puig, the lawyer."

"*Sí?*"

"I wondered if I could call round to see you today."

"Not today," Jack said. He was going to add that he had company, but decided on a minimalist approach to the conversation.

"Well, we can speak now. I wanted to ask you something about your house," he said in the clipped, business-like kind of voice that Jack had never liked. Here was a PP – the conservative party – adherent for sure.

"Yes?"

"I don't know if you've ever considered selling it."

"No."

"No you haven't?"

"No."

"And would you?"

"No."

"Right. In case you ever reconsider I'd be prepared to offer you €135,000 for it." Jack made no reply. "Would you consider that offer? It's a generous one."

Jack decided to drop his monosyllabic manner in order to gather information. "As I say, it's not for sale, so you can tell Les to look elsewhere."

"Les? Oh, that *inglés*. No, no, I speak on behalf of no-one."

"No-one?"

"Or rather, on behalf of myself."

"You could get a bigger house with a pool for that price at the moment."

"Yes, but I like the… situation of the house."

"Me too. Who gave you my number?"

"Er… well, it was Adán Martínez, the builder."

"Oh yes, the one who has a terrible reputation."

"Yes… no, I don't know… It was just a chance meeting."

"Tell Les that I wouldn't sell him the house for a million euros."

"But it's not Les-"

"*Adiós*," Jack said, and hung up.

Jack switched off the phone and began to flick through his book. He would get the roof looked at first, then the wiring and plumbing. They could get on with ripping up the old floor tiles while he was waiting for those things to be seen to. The new windows would have to go in soon, which would get one big expense out of the way.

His mind went back to the conversation with Néstor. Perhaps he shouldn't have hung up on him, or not so soon at any rate. Did he really want the house for himself, or was it just a ruse? Well, let them keep bidding against, or with, each other. He surveyed his land and looked down the length of his porch, before gazing at the hills across the valley. Yes, it was fine here, but if Les was prepared to pay over the odds for Josemi's old house, what would he pay for this one? If he reached two hundred thousand he'd have to give it some serious thought; there was his old age to think about, after all.

* * *

"Hello, Néstor," said Les from the sunbed as he saw the slight, dapper man approaching. "Pull up a chair and Denise will get you a drink."

"What would you both like?" Denise asked as she sat up and stretched.

"A whisky and water for me, dear."

"The same for me please, Denise, but not too strong," said Néstor as he pulled a wicker chair up close to Les's sunbed. "It's not so hot for sunbathing now."

"Oh, we sunbathe most of the year," said Denise, squeezing her feet into her sandals. "And it's nice to relax after lunch."

"Nothing else to do until we get this project underway," said Les gruffly. "So, it seems that this Josemi character is especially averse to selling that old house to me."

"That's what the last words of our conversation yesterday led me to believe, yes," said Néstor, ever the diplomat.

"There's nothing wrong with our money," said Denise over her shoulder as she waddled towards the house.

"I can't understand his attitude," said Néstor to Les. "Either he's got a job or he has received some money; that's the only explanation. Thirty thousand is an excellent price for that house now, compared to what else you can buy for the money."

"He'll come round, but if not you'll have to find me another house that Brian can do up. If he finds his own work I won't be sure that he's not employing Jack."

"Oh, I have my informers," said Néstor. "But I'm sure I can find another old house for sale in the village."

"You do that. As for Jack's house, I'll offer him a bit more soon. The longer he's out of work, the more likely he is to see sense."

"I think so. Nobody else will offer as much as you did at the present time. The man didn't appreciate your generosity."

"No, sometimes people don't."

Denise returned with the whiskies and a Malibu and coke for herself.

"Thanks, dear." Les took a long drink. "Ah, that's refreshing. Where are you up to with old Pedro?" he asked Néstor.

"Persevering. I spoke to his son Pedrito yesterday and he says that his father is considering dividing the land into four parts. He thinks his brothers and sisters may sell, but he would not be allowed to sell while the old man is still around."

"Which hopefully won't be for too long, if he's as ill as you say he is."

"Quite ill, yes."

"Still, if I can get hold of some of his land, and Jack's house, we can make a start. It'd be convenient if Pedro's son's quarter of the land was the furthest away, if we can't get it until the old man pops his clogs."

"Pops his what?"

"Clogs. Kicks the bucket. Dies."

"Oh, yes, that would be the best plan," said Néstor, marvelling at the naivety of this grotesque *inglés*. Did he think things were so easy? Did he think he could buy whatever he wanted? Who was to say that the others would want to sell? The Spanish know the value of land and are loath to part with it. If Pedrito's siblings were doing well they might not be so easily persuaded. As for Jack, well, he was proving to be a tougher customer than expected. He wasn't at all like other English people he had come across, to whom a house was just a commodity which they would sell if they thought the money would get them something bigger and better. No, this Jack was more like a Spaniard, not so easily uprooted from a place where he felt at home. The fat man sprawled before him guzzling whisky had had a good idea, there was no doubt of that, but he might not be the best person to execute the plan.

"A penny for your thoughts, Néstor." said Les.

"What? Oh, I was just thinking about this man Jack. He seems – from what you say – to be very... stubborn."

"Yes, but I've bought out small haulage firms from folk more stubborn than him. Everyone has their price. I'll offer him €135,000 next week."

"Would you like me to communicate this to him? If I study the market a little and point out to him some properties that he can buy for that money, he may be more easily persuaded."

"Right, yes, you speak to him from now on. I'm not used to talking to folk who don't see reason."

"I will take care of everything," said Néstor, smiling broadly when Les leant over to nudge his dozing wife.

"How about another whisky, dear?"

Sundays were rarely days of rest for Néstor and as he drove down the motorway to Alicante he called Martínez on his hands-free phone. After many rings, he answered.

"Adán? It's Néstor."

"Oh, I was asleep. What is it?"

"I just wanted to fill you in on the latest developments."

"Could it not have waited until tomorrow?"

"Tomorrow morning I have a meeting in Alicante with a potential backer."

"A backer? Of what?"

"The Englishman's project, of course."

"I thought he was financing it himself."

Néstor heard the click of a lighter and waited for the nicotine to reactivate the dozy builder's brain. "Just because he had the idea, it doesn't necessarily mean that he gets to carry it out. The man I'm meeting tomorrow has far more financial weight than Les, and I've already begun to convince him that this project is a winner."

"But is it? Nobody's building anything like that nowadays."

"Yes, for seven years nobody has built. Many of the *urbanizaciones* that didn't sell are now so decrepit that they don't appeal to the new influx of foreign buyers. I've seen this for myself down on the coast. They see a jungle of weeds and boarded up bars and shops and no matter how much the estate agents try to convince them that it will all be restored to its former beauty, they walk away. People want new houses, not old new houses."

"I'd love to get back to building houses. I've got plenty of work, but it's all renovation work."

"That is the reason for my call, Adán. When I sit down with this man tomorrow, can I tell him that I have a builder who is capable of building six or seven luxury houses with pools within two years?"

"Of course you can. I can get workers in from miles around if necessary."

"And can I tell him that the cost of the houses will not be excessive?"

"Oh, I know what the foreigners look for. They want good windows and doors, good tiling, finishing, and a pretty pool. I can build beautiful houses out of breeze blocks, you know, and guarantee no subsidence for... quite some time."

"There must be no subsidence or cracks until the last of the houses is sold."

"Exactly. You can count on me, Néstor. So is this Les out of the picture?"

"Not at all. He thinks he is the driving force and we may still have to fall back on him, but I don't think he realises how much he will have to spend to buy Pedro's land and Jack's house. Tomorrow I will know if the new backer is prepared to make offers that they cannot refuse."

"I asked Jack to come to work for me, you know, but *he* refused."

"Try again. He could be useful to us and will eventually sell."

"Do we really need his house?" Martínez asked, now wide awake.

"Yes, we do. I envisage the show house on that spot and the other houses will be accessed by a road going along the side of the land."

"If the council gives permission."

"Ha, if they give permission. That's one more reason why I prefer the new backer. He will understand that there will be councillors to be… appeased. The repulsive Englishman may not understand that additional expense as he is not used to our ways. Tomorrow could be the start of something big for you and me, Adán."

"Yes. I take it the new backer is Spanish then?"

"No, better than that. He is Russian."

* * *

"Les? Hello, it's Brian here."

"Hi, Brian. Just a minute." Les pushed himself up from the sunbed and put on his shirt. He drained his glass and picked up the phone. "How's it going?"

"Not bad. I was just wondering when we'd be starting work on that old house in the village."

"Well, the owner, a bloke called Josemi or some daft name like that, is being a bit… troublesome."

"So he's not selling?"

"He *thinks* he's not selling, but I've still got Néstor on his case," Les said, before belching softly. "Mind you, if that bloody lawyer doesn't get his finger out I'll be firing him. He's done sod all so far except talk the talk."

"Right."

"But don't worry, if I don't get that house I'll get another one, I'm determined to get… to get an old house in the village. Are things a bit quiet or something?"

"Very. I've been sort of counting on starting the job soon."

"You will, you will. Take a week off and enjoy yourself, ha ha. I'll be in touch soon."

"What did he say, Brian?" asked Liz before the phone had touched the table.

"I think he was drunk. He hasn't bought the house yet and says that if he can't get that one he'll look for another to buy." Brian shook his head and avoided his wife's wide, blazing eyes.

"What the hell are we supposed to *do* then?" she yelled.

"Calm down, love. I've got one or two little jobs to do that I've been putting off."

"Like what?" she asked in an ominously low voice.

"The Bensons want me to gravel their driveway."

"Oh, big bloody deal!" she shrieked. "That'll hardly keep us in cornflakes."

Brian put his hand over his eyes and sighed. There was no use mentioning that it had been her idea for him to throw his lot in with Les, not in her current frame of mind. During the last week their home had been so full of her grand designs for their future that he had started to believe in Les's great plan and hadn't been touting for work as he usually did. A driveway to gravel, a small poolside wall to build, and then what? Since he had stopped counting on Jack his luck seemed to have deserted him.

"I'll have a drive around tomorrow and see if anyone needs anything doing."

"I never did trust that fat bastard Les," she muttered, wiping away a tear.

"Oh, he's all right. He'll come through in the end. Do you fancy a drink?"

"Vodka."

"With?"

"Ice."

11

Jack spent Monday and Tuesday at home with his mobile phone switched off, only turning it on from time to time to see if he had missed a call from Salvador, Vicente, Josemi, or anybody else unlikely to perturb him. He needed some time out from recent events in order to take stock of his situation and he spent both days working on his land, cleaning, cooking, reading and thinking.

During this time his thoughts regarding the turn his life had taken fluctuated from mild euphoria to mild despondency, the nadir arriving at dusk on Tuesday as he sat on the porch wearing a jacket for the first time since spring. Why had he got himself involved in such a risky, bothersome scheme? Why had he not just looked for some building work himself? He could do most of the jobs he had been doing with Brian on his own now and there would have been nothing to stop him cutting in and even undercutting his old employer. Why not? Because it was, or soon would be, time to get out of the building game. So what does the bright spark do? He buys a whole house to restore. Brilliant.

Still, the old back had been no trouble lately and with Josemi's help the restoration work shouldn't be too taxing. No walls to build, no beams to lift and put in place. No, the work would be all right, but what about the animosity his acquisition might create?

"I've lived too quietly for too long," he said to the black cat asleep on the chair next to his. "Now I either pull out and hole myself up here, or I get stuck in and just ignore any pillocks who don't like what I've done."

He went to pour himself a glass of the good brandy and returned to the porch. At least by putting all his eggs in the one bricks and mortar basket he wouldn't have to bother trying to sell houses. That idea really was a non-starter for anyone who didn't like mixing with people.

"I should be thankful for small mercies," he said to the still nameless cat that opened one eye and closed it again.

* * *

"You've done what? Bought a house?" asked Vicente the next day as they drank coffee at a table in the corner of Mario's almost deserted bar. He had come straight from work and his uniform made the question sound like an accusation.

"Keep your voice down, it's still a secret. So what do you think?"

"I'm still trying to assimilate what you've told me, Jack. Let's get this straight." He lowered his voice. "You've just agreed to buy the house for seven thousand more than Josemi had been offered?"

"Yes, but I knew that Les would increase his offer," he replied, half truthfully.

"Which he did, by a lot. I don't know who's dafter, you or Josemi."

"Josemi has honoured our agreement," Jack said before tapping the table with his knuckles.

"And I admire him for it. I always thought of him as a bit of a wastrel, always on the *tragaperras*."

"Not any more." Jack tapped the table again and smiled. "And he's going to work on the house with me, before you mention my back."

"Hmm, he knows his stuff. I don't think your purchase such a bad idea. You'll make at least a little money, maybe quite a bit. Anyway, speaking of houses, I've found out who is interested in buying yours."

"Thanks for asking, but I already know."

"I don't know how you know. I asked my chief suspect directly and his face gave him away. He then begged me to keep it a secret. Perhaps I should have been a detective after all," he said, brushing invisible dust from his sleeve.

"I thought you couldn't speak English."

"English? Why would I speak to Marco in English? He struggles with Spanish, the brute."

"Marco? The baker?"

"Who else?"

"Bloody hell," Jack said in English.

"Meaning?"

"*Caramba*, I thought it was just Les, a fat *inglés*, and Néstor Puig, and maybe Martínez."

"Have you struck oil while digging up turnips or something?"

"You'd think so." Jack went on to give Vicente a brief account of recent events, *sotto voce*, much to Mario's annoyance. Mario only liked secrets if he was in on them. "So that's the story so far, or it was until you told me about Marco being interested in the house too."

"Hmm, given what you've just told me it sounds like the gossip has reached Marco in a much embellished state and he now thinks that your house is the Taj Mahal."

"A mausoleum? It will be if they don't leave me in peace."

"You know what I mean. Mario! Two small brandies over here, please."

"Yes, officer. Right away, officer," said Mario, saluting.

Bringing over the brandies gave Mario a much desired excuse to join the conversation. "You two look like you're plotting to overthrow the king," he said, flicking a grey dishcloth over his shoulder.

"Just telling Jack about my dancing exploits," said Vicente, twirling his fingers in the air.

"Ha, I bet, but don't worry, I know most of what goes on in this village, including something that will be news to you, Jack. Can I speak in front of this man in the foreign uniform?"

"I'm on my way home, Mario," said Vicente.

"Our charming pair of *guardia civiles* will not be pleased if they see you dressed like that, and armed, on their territory."

"Those two? Ha, whenever there's anything to do here they're round at my flat asking my advice."

"Luckily we live in a crime-free *pueblo* and have no need for *policía local* too," Mario said.

"What were you going to say, Mario?" asked Jack. "You may speak freely in front of this enemy agent."

"Hmm, I can tell you in broad terms, but not the details. The people involved, as I explained to you last week, do not wish their... desires to be known," said Mario, smiling at an uncomprehending Vicente. Jack's face suggested that he wasn't too clear about what he meant either. "Jack, you remember what we discussed the last time you were here?"

"Oh, yes."

"I already have four, possibly five people who would like to enlist your services."

"Right." Jack sipped his brandy. "I'd almost forgotten about that."

"I can give you the details when we are alone together." Mario winked at Jack, raised his eyebrows to Vicente, and returned to the bar.

"What was that about?" asked Vicente on observing Jack's worried expression.

"Oh, you remember the house selling idea that Salva suggested? Mario has been looking into it for me."

"Ah, I see. With some success, it appears."

"Yes, but now that I'm going to be starting work on the house, I'd rather not bother with any of that."

"Why not? If you'll be in the village anyway it costs nothing to speak to them and take a look at the properties."

"That's true, but finding buyers is a different matter. That would take time, and effort."

"You mentioned €1000 for a house sale."

"Yes, that was the idea."

"Sell one and you can give Josemi, what? Eleven or twelve days work?"

"That's true."

"Make money, finish the house, sell it, and then you can return to your tranquil existence."

"A tranquil existence, yes, that's all I really want."

"I shall leave you to speak to Mario alone now. Call me if you need anything."

"Thanks, Vicente."

When Vicente's boots hit the pavement Mario came over flourishing a sheet of paper.

"Here is a list of the people, their telephone numbers, and details of the properties they want to sell."

"Thanks, Mario." Jack held out his hand for the sheet but Mario kept it pressed against his chest.

"Yes, the response has been very good. People seem to trust you here, despite you being an outsider."

Jack thought about the intrigues and petty jealousies he had heard about over the years and concluded that they might trust him *because* he was an outsider.

"You will see," Mario went on, "that I have done my work thoroughly. Against each name I have written their asking price *and*..." He raised a chubby index finger. "...the price for which *I* think they will sell."

"Thanks, Mario," Jack said, keeping both hands on the table. "Don't worry, I haven't forgotten our agreement – 10% of the commission for you."

Mario lowered the sheet almost to within Jack's reach. "But *that* must remain our little secret." Jack nodded and was finally allowed to grasp Mario's report.

He scanned the list of five names and was pleased to see that he knew two of them only vaguely and three not at all. He thought that Juanma Tortosa was probably Reme the newsagent's brother and María Jesús Muñoz might be Jaime the joiner's aunt, or even his mother. He folded the sheet and slid it into his shirt pocket.

"Aren't you going to ring them?" asked Mario, still hovering by the table.

"Later, when I've analysed your data. Give me the bill, please, and I'll be off."

"No charge, *compadre*."

"Thanks, Mario." Jack got to his feet and had made it half way to the door before the inevitable question came.

"Oh, and did you speak to Josemi?"

Jack stopped in his tracks and turned round. "Yes, we had a chat."

Mario took his usual histrionic precaution of walking to the door and looking up and down the street. "Why did you want to speak to him?" he asked, eyes wide with anticipation.

"Well..." Jack thought quickly and saw no point in keeping the house sale a secret any longer. Salvador had confirmed that morning that the survey had been done, the contract discussed with Josemi and Esperanza, and an appointment made at the notary's office for the following week. "I'm buying the house."

Mario's eyes bulged to the limits of their sockets and his face broke into a smile that revealed most of his off-white teeth, gold fillings and all. "So you outbid the fat *inglés*?"

Jack moved his head from side to side, meaning 'maybe' in Spain.

"Tell me all, Jack."

"I'm sworn to secrecy about the price, I'm afraid, but I'm going to restore the house and Josemi is going to work with me on the project until he starts working for himself in November."

'More news!' Mario's eyes said, but he stuck to the day's main headline. "And your purchase of the house? Is that to be kept secret too?"

Mario's expression was such an imploring one that Jack threw caution to the wind. Everyone would know soon enough, anyway. "No, you can tell whoever you like."

Mario looked at his watch and Jack looked at his. 6.45pm. Post-work beers would soon be flowing. He had a quarter of an hour to get out of the village.

12

"He's done *what*?"

"He's bought the old house from Josemi, Les." Néstor cradled the phone with his shoulder and arranged some papers on his desk. "One of my… friends just phoned to tell me. Are you still there, Les?"

"I'm here, but how the hell did he do that?"

"He outbid you, I expect."

"But how?"

"By offering more money."

"Don't be funny, Néstor, I know that. I thought he was supposed to be piss poor?"

"Piss poor?"

"*Very* poor. You really must work on your English. So, what are you going to do about it?"

"Me?"

"Yes, you. Why do you think I'm paying you six hundred a month?"

"My consultation fee? Well, to get the benefit of my advice."

"And what *is* your advice?" Les asked, ill pleased by the lawyer's nonchalant tone.

"Well, as we discussed, we could find another old house for Brian to restore, but as the whole object of that tactic was to starve Jack into submission... is that good English?"

"Yes, yes, have a gold star, but go on."

"Well, as Jack appears to be nowhere near starving, that manoeuvre now seems to be redundant."

"True, so what next?"

"There's only one thing left to do. Make Jack an offer he cannot refuse."

"I'd planned to up my offer to 135,000, as you know."

"Hmm, if he has paid... perhaps thirty-five thousand for that old house, you may need to go higher."

"One fifty?"

"I would make a final and definitive offer; two hundred with up to half of it in cash."

"Bloody hell, Néstor! I'm not made of money... Néstor?"

"I'm thinking." He watched his new secretary enter the room and place a cup of coffee on his desk. Pretty, excellent body, but no class. No, she would never become Señora Puig.

"Hello?" Les tapped the phone on the solid oak kitchen table and put it back to his ear.

"This is my analysis of the situation, Les. We are embarking on a project which will require large expenditure in order to obtain large rewards. If you... if we cannot overcome the first barrier – the small matter of expropriating Jack – how can we proceed? Pedro Poveda's family will not sell cheaply, you know, and there is also the matter of certain... incentives for the council members so that they will allow us to build the desired number of houses on the land and lay access roads where we wish."

"Incentives? Oh, I can manage a few bottles of champagne all right."

"Bottles of champagne? No, no, the councillors will require something even more liquid than champagne."

"Money? How much?"

"Well, the best tactic would be to approach the PP councillors first. They will all be agreeable – I can guarantee that – but, being conservatives, they have expensive tastes. Then we will need two more votes. I think Soler, the Valencia Party councillor will be... pliable, and I know that Juan Molina, who is independent, wishes to plant new olive trees."

"Bloody hell, it sounds like Russia or something."

"Russia? Why do you say Russia?"

"Oh, because of all the mafias there."

"Ah."

"So, how much?"

"At a conservative estimate, I think that sixty or seventy thousand should cover it, maybe a little more."

"What?!"

"If we approached the Socialist councillors it would be even more expensive. They have more scruples, you see."

"Why did you not mention this before, Néstor?" Les filled his coffee cup to the brim with brandy, one of the few Spanish habits he had acquired.

"I wanted to take things one step at a time. Your first objective was Jack's house, so I concentrated on that. If that's not possible... well, I don't know."

"Are you getting cold feet, Néstor?"

"Cold feet? Ah, I see. No, I am as motivated as ever, but I must have guarantees of your financial... potency." Néstor smiled and lit a cigarette.

"I see your point. Well, I've just thought of one way to increase my financial... potency."

"What's that, Les?"

"By firing you, you little arsehole. *Adiós*."

"Fancy hearing you speaking the lingo," said Denise as she entered the kitchen in her billowing nightie.

"I've just fired Néstor."

"Oh, what's he done?"

"Just given me a load of bullshit, for a start. He said I should offer Jack two hundred grand and that I'll also have to shell out a fortune to bribe the bloody councillors."

"What for?"

"To get permission to build. You can't just build anywhere, you know."

"Don't be snappy, Les, and put that brandy away. It's only half past nine. What are you going to do now?"

"Think." He topped up his cup.

"Think, not drink," Denise said, screwing the bottle top on. "Perhaps we should forget about the whole thing."

"No spic or northerner is going to make a fool of me, Denise, I can tell you that."

"No dear, but to be fair to Jack, not selling you his house is hardly making a fool of you. It is his, after all."

"Hmph."

"I'll make you some bacon and eggs."

* * *

Adán Martínez had just given his men instructions regarding the extension they were building for an English couple in a tiny hamlet not far from the village and was driving to a roadside bar for breakfast. Sending his son, also Adán, off to learn English and inundating the villages with bilingual leaflets and business cards was starting to pay off. This couple would be out to inspect the job a month from now. If he worked fast enough they would never know that the double thickness brick walls with insulation that they were paying for were in fact breeze blocks. Martínez loved breeze blocks. So cheap, so easy to build with. One of the more cynical workers said that his boss's tomb should be made of them as a monument to his greed, but of course Martínez didn't know that. He paid his workers well on the condition that they worked like demons. No time for succulent bar breakfasts for them and he had got them out of the habit of long lunches too. If they didn't like it they could go to work for... ha! For whom? He was the only builder in the area with more than a couple of men and his employees knew that.

He ordered a steak, red pepper and mushroom bocadillo, a small salad, olives, and red wine with lemonade. This was the life. The walls would have risen a good way by the time he got back or his men would know about it. When he started this project of Néstor's he'd have his work cut out, but he didn't mind spending more time on site if there was money in it, and boy would there be money in it. When he had finished eating and ordered his coffee and brandy he phoned the lawyer.

"Any news, Néstor?"

"Lots. I was going to ring you later. The latest is that Les has sacked me."

"Sacked you?"

"That's what the fat fool called it. I spelt out to him what he would need to do and he didn't like it."

"Bad news then."

"Bad? No, irrelevant. The Russian backer I met on Monday came up to take a look yesterday and is very keen. He has a *lot* of black money to get rid of and what better way to do it than by building houses?"

"If they sell, yes. Are you so sure that people will buy them? I still think it's a bit soon."

"Things are looking better than ever. Not only have we got the fat man's instinct that the English will buy them, but now we might well have Russian buyers too. There are plenty more like the backer who want a little nest here."

"The Red Army invading inland Alicante, eh?"

"There's nothing red about this lot. Mafiosos, more like."

"Well, we must encourage enterprise. So, the first thing will be to get Jack's house, I suppose."

"Yes, I guess you've heard the news."

"What's that?"

"That he's gone and bought Josemi's house."

"Him? Jack? I though he was penniless?"

"Apparently not, but no matter. We'll just have to pay more for his house."

"Hmm, so he's not as dumb as you thought, Néstor?"

"No, he stands to come out of it very well, but we can afford to share our good fortune, a little. I shall be making him an offer he cannot refuse very soon."

Martínez drained his brandy glass. "And I'm ready to start work any time."

* * *

When Brian and his son arrived home from the day's gravelling Josh went straight upstairs to his room without a word to his mother. Brian envied that prerogative of adolescence as he took off his boots in the hallway and prepared to greet his wife as cheerily as he could. On top of all his other problems the boy wasn't taking to building work very well at all and having him rake gravel in the sun for six hours was hardly likely to endear him to the trade. Perhaps they should send him off to college to study something else – like mechanics, because he was keen on cars – but that would cost money and they had little to spare at the moment.

Being self-employed in Spain was all very well when there was plenty of work, but the monthly payments of over €250 were a lead weight when things were slow. The previous month Brian hadn't earned a cent for himself until the second week and the rest of the month had been no bonanza either. He had thought that by letting Jack go he would be better off, but it seemed to have put a curse on him. If only Les would buy that house, or another one like it. He knew that the scheming so-and-so's motives were all wrong, but it was getting to a point where he had to think about number one. Jack would be all right. He didn't need much to get by and was lucky enough not to be married.

"Hello, dear, I'm back," he said as he entered the living room. The television was on loud – yet another cookery programme – and Liz's glazed expression suggested that the transparent liquid in her glass was not water. "Are you all right?"

"I will be next week," her lips appeared to say.

Brian turned the sound down. "What's happening next week? Has Les rung with any news?"

"No, I rang Denise."

"And?"

"That old house that *you* were going to be doing up."

"What about it?"

"That sneaky bastard Jack has gone and bought it, that's all."

"Jack? Are you sure?"

"Do I look *stupid*?" she shouted. She took a drink and her bloodshot blue eyes looked at Brian for the first time. "Denise told me that Néstor told Les about it," she said in a seething voice. "She also told me that Les has sacked Néstor and has spent all day *thinking*, as he calls it."

Brian went into the kitchen and was back with a can of beer within a minute. He sat down next to Liz on the sofa and opened the can. "So why will we be all right next week?"

"*I* will be. I'm going back to England."

"To visit your mother?"

"To stay. I'm finished here." She burst into tears.

Brian reached out his hand but thought better of it. "For goodness sake, Liz, this is only a blip. I've done all right for years up to this last month or two. Things'll pick up, you'll see."

"Things'll pick up. I'm sick of hearing those words. Just when it looked like you were finally getting somewhere and this happens. Of all the devious bastards, that Jack beats them all."

"Jack's not like that. He must have had a good reason," Brian said, fairly sure of what it was. "I'll talk to him. I'll talk to Les too."

"Fat lot of good that'll do. Denise says Les might have his black dog."

"What's that?"

"It's what Churchill used to get. Depression. She says he might not come out of it for weeks, so he'll be no use. You'll have to talk to Jack though."

"I will, but-"

"Ask him for work."

Brian stared at his wife before drinking half of the beer. "Ask Jack for work? But... but if he wanted my help he'd have told me."

"Ask him for work. No, *tell* him to give you some work. You've given him enough, haven't you?"

Brian finished the beer and crumpled the can slowly. "Listen, tomorrow I'll drive round and visit all the people I know and ask about work. There are always new folk coming out and somebody will tip me off about a good job, I'm sure. If nothing comes up, I'll ring Jack tomorrow evening. How's that?"

"Hmm," she said with a shrug.

"So you'll stay?"

"What day is it?"

"Thursday."

"I shan't book my flight until the weekend."

13

Jack had planned to spend Thursday clearing away some of the summer crops, but the sheet of paper that Mario had given him caught his eye every time he passed the kitchen table. After lunch and with little work left to do he took it, a pen and his phone out to the porch with his coffee and tried to muster some enthusiasm for the task ahead. He hated phoning people he didn't know, but they would presumably be expecting a call. Of the five names on the list one was only a maybe, so he crossed it out faintly, sure that Mario would tell him when they made their mind up to sell.

He called Juanma Tortosa first. He turned out to be Reme the newsagent's uncle and told Jack that he had a plot of land big enough to build on that he wished to sell.

"But I'll not sell to anyone from the village. It'll have to be a foreigner or someone from out of the area," he said in the hoarse voice of an older man.

"Why's that, if you don't mind me asking?"

"Because I'm not having someone else work my land. They can build on it, but I don't want to see anyone else's tractor on there. It's been in the family for as long as anyone can remember, but none of the young ones are interested. I'll sell it and get myself a nice car while I'm still young enough to drive it."

Jack made some notes on the size and location of the land and promised to look for a non-agricultural buyer.

"You do that, Jack, but not a word in the village, eh?"

"Don't worry about that, Juanma, but it would be best to remind Mario to keep quiet about it."

"I've already told him that if word gets out I'll chop his balls off."

"Ha, right. One thing though; whoever buys it won't be building on all of it. They're bound to want to plant something."

"Oh, I don't mind them playing at it, I just don't want another *agricultor* taking it over. I'd be driving past thinking it was still mine. No, a fence round it and a house, that's what I want to see."

"I'll do what I can."

Jack sipped his coffee and keyed in another number. The sooner he got it over with, the better.

"Señora Muñoz? This is Jack, the *inglés*, here."

"Hola. Mario said you'd be calling. It's about the house, isn't it?"

"Yes. Are you Jaime's aunt?"

"That's right," she said, sounding pleased. "I have eight nephews and nieces, as well as three of my own."

"Ah, how nice. Are none of them interested in the house?"

"Uf, no. Most of them live away and none of them like old houses anyway. It seems like only foreigners want them anymore."

"It does seem that way, yes. All I'm doing, Señora Muñoz, is, er, connecting people who want to buy and sell. I know a lot of foreigners who are looking for houses, you see," he said, cringing at his little fib.

"Call me María Jesús. You're as old as me, after all. I've seen you about the village on your bike."

It crossed Jack's mind that he should really arrange to meet her and the others, but as he didn't have a single buyer lined up, he had thought of putting it off until more auspicious times. Then again, if he didn't see the properties he would have trouble describing them.

"Can we meet up one day to take a look at the house, María Jesús?"

"Whenever you want. Just call and I'll meet you. It's a big old thing and needs a lot of work doing on it."

"That's how some foreigners like them."

"Yes. So, Mario tells me that you only charge €1000."

"That's right," he said, as if he were a veteran of many sales. "I'm only introducing sellers to buyers, after all." He cringed again. Fool, he thought, you should make it sound like a complicated process.

"Well, you're cheaper than these estate agents. I think young Marta charges a percentage. I was going to talk to her but I don't really want photos of the house in her window so that all the village will know that I'm selling. I'd rather do it quietly and it's nobody's business how much I sell it for, is it?"

"No, it isn't. I'll call you when I'm in the village and we'll take a look at it."

"You do that."

Two down, three to go, he thought, as he went inside to refill his coffee cup. Someone called Juan, third on the list, didn't answer, so he put a little cross against his name and phoned the next.

"Hola, Pablo?" he said, wondering why he only called women by their surnames. "It's Jack here, the *inglés* who Mario might have mentioned to you."

"Who?"

"Jack. I'm ringing about the house that Mario said you wanted to sell."

"Ah, yes. Are you the one who's bought that house of Josemi's?" he asked in what Jack thought to be a rather accusing manner.

"Er, yes, that's me."

"Buying up the village, eh?"

If only you knew why I've bought it, Jack thought. "Ha, no, no, just that one. It's for some friends of mine." Heck, you soon start lying when you get into this game, he thought. No wonder most estate agents ended up with a reputation for it.

"And I believe you're selling your house out in the country," Pablo said, convincing Jack that he was one of those silent, retired men who spend most of the day in the bars gathering gossip.

"No, who told you that?"

"Oh, I just heard it mentioned."

"No, I'm definitely not selling mine. That's where I plan to end my days," he added to make things crystal clear. Go tell your sources that, he thought.

"So, you can sell mine, can you… Jack?"

"I might be able to, yes."

"Without anyone in the village knowing?"

"Not from me, they won't. I can promise you that," Jack said, the image of Mario's goggling eyes flashing through his mind.

"And no-one will find out the price either?"

"Not from me. I put you in touch with the buyer. If it goes through, you pay me the €1000 fee and that's that," he said, adopting the man's terse tone.

"Right. It's an old house down near the sports ground."

"Can we go and see it sometime?"

"Not together we can't. If they see me with you they'll know I'm selling it. It's four doors up from the sports ground."

"Can you be more precise, Pablo?"

"It's the only one with green window frames; what's left of them, anyway."

"Right, I'll just walk past one day and have a quick look," Jack said. He didn't like this man and had little desire to help him to sell his house. He seemed just the kind who would vacillate when it came to paying the commission.

"Don't you want to see inside it?"

"I'll have a look from the outside first."

"I'll leave the key with Mario, but don't let anyone see you go in."

"OK, Pablo, you do that," he said before sticking his tongue out at the phone. "I'll be in touch."

Jack dropped the phone onto the table and looked at the sky. Dark clouds were gathering, but if he got the last call over with he should just have time to pull up the old watermelon vines before the heavens opened.

"Hola, Encarna?" he said, deciding to dispense with formalities. "It's Jack here, the *inglés* who Mario might have mentioned to you."

"Ah, the cycling *guiri*," said the youngest voice so far.

"I suppose so, yes."

"I'm joking. You're practically one of us now," she said in a pleasant sing-song voice. "Anyway, the house I want to sell was my mother's. She died earlier this year."

"I'm sorry to hear that."

"Thanks. She was almost eighty and had been ill for some time. She was ready to go, really."

Jack, to his surprise, found himself trying to guess Encarna's age. She could be as old as him, but sounded younger. Fifty perhaps? He liked her voice and was glad he'd left her till last. "So, er... can we meet sometime and take a look at the house, Encarna?"

"Whenever you want, Jack. It's not a bad place. It's old, but the windows and doors are fairly new. It's near Ramón's hardware shop, three doors further up."

"We could meet one evening, when it's quiet."

"Whenever. Oh, I don't mind who knows I'm selling it. Mario was going on about keeping it a secret, the clown, but it's only a house, after all," she said with a giggle that made Jack wonder what she looked like. She *sounded* pretty. She even sounded slimmer than most of the middle-aged women of the village, but how on earth he thought he could tell that he didn't know.

"I'll call you one day next week then," he said.

"You do that, Jack. I look forward to meeting you."

"Likewise. *Adiós*, Encarna."

"Ciao, Jack."

By the time he had ripped up the watermelon vines and dragged them over to the pile of vegetation to be burnt the first heavy drops of rain had begun to pepper the dry earth. He walked back to the porch, changed from espadrilles to sandals, and picked up Mario's sheet, now also covered with his own notes. He would take a look at Juanma's land on his way to Monóvar to visit the bank tomorrow and he could arrange to see María Jesús's house on returning to the village; maybe Pablo's too if the old buzzard had left the key at Mario's. For some reason he had told Encarna that he would call her next week, so he ought to stick to that plan.

"But why?" he said only to himself, as the black cat was nowhere to be seen. "Not playing hard to get, are we?" He laughed aloud at his unfamiliar reaction to the sound of an attractive woman's voice; the voice, not necessarily the woman, because she might be ugly, fat or wall-eyed. She might even be married – he hadn't thought of that – but he had a feeling that she wasn't.

He chuckled and told himself not to get his hopes up. If she was anything like most of the women he knew she would spend hours watching tripe on television and hours more at interminable meals with friends and relatives. Where did a man like him fit into that kind of lifestyle? Having said that, he couldn't remember hearing her voice at any of the raucous morning get-togethers at Julio's bar. She had sounded different, but, all the same, it would be best to put her out of his mind, at least until next week. Whatever happened, it was still nice to have got that old feeling again, a feeling he hadn't had since his short-lived fling with Esme all those years ago. He wasn't past it just yet.

14

Whenever Jack had to use the car he always liked to pack as many errands into the outing as possible, so before he set off to the bank he put all three of his gas bottles in the boot. The *bombona* which had lasted him all summer wasn't quite empty, but by changing all three for full ones they might well last him through the winter. He had a wood-burning stove for the really cold weather, but there was still plenty of wood from last winter's delivery. You could really keep the bills down in Spain if you were careful and Jack wondered how much more they would be in Accrington. Hopefully he would never have to find out.

He parked outside Ramón's hardware store and realised that he would be paying many a visit to the building section next door in the coming weeks. Brian had always bought the materials they used, but he knew well enough what he would need. He carried two bottles into the shop and was on his way outside for the third when Pam came in struggling with a *bombona* of her own.

"Hi, Pam," he said as he relieved her of the burden. "Have they stopped delivering in the village, or what?"

"No, but I need this one right now," she said in the Shropshire accent that he had always liked. She wiped a bead of sweat from her temple and stood with her hands on her ample hips.

"I'll get my other one and then I'll help you get yours into the car," said Jack. "Ramón! Four *bombonas* over here, please."

"Right away, Jack," said the pale, plump owner, whose prosperity had kept him busy indoors for the last few years. "Juanito! Four *bombonas* out here quick," he said to a gangly lad who stood prodding his phone behind the counter. "I expect I'll be seeing you in the other half of the shop soon, eh?"

"Why's that Ramón? What have you heard?"

"Oh, that you're selling your house and moving into the one you've bought from Josemi."

"Is that true, Jack?" asked Pam in her halting but correct Spanish.

"No, it is *not* true," he said to them both. "Who told you I was selling my house, Ramón?"

"Oh, someone mentioned it in Julio's."

"Who, if you don't mind me asking?" Jack asked, striving to keep his voice as pleasant as possible.

"Oh, Martínez, I think. Yes, I heard him say something about you being bound to sell eventually." He observed Jack's face. "Have I said something wrong?"

"Not wrong, no, just mistaken. Josemi's house is not for me and my house is not for sale. How much do I owe you?"

"Er, that'll be... €52.50."

"It's not getting any cheaper, is it?"

"They say the price might fall a bit soon. Just one for you, Pam?"

"Yes please, Ramón."

"I was planning to pay you a visit later," Jack said to Pam in English. He knew it was a rude thing to do, but he desired no more gossip from Ramón and wished him to know it.

"A likely story. We haven't had a proper chat for ages."

"No, but it's true. I'm driving over to Monóvar now and I'll call in on the way back."

"You do that, Jack."

After they had paid Ramón, Jack lugged all the gas bottles to their cars and Pam set off back to her bar. Jack closed his boot and wandered up the street. Three doors up from Ramón's, Encarna had said. It was a large, white, two-storey house and the dust on the double-glazed windows convinced him that it was the one. No self-respecting village woman would let a single mote of dust stay on her downstairs windows for more than an hour. He walked across the street to take a look at the roof. It looked sound and the house had been painted within the last few years. This was no ruin and he doubted that it needed much doing to it at all. Well, there must be some foreigners around who wanted to move straight in. Next week, on Monday perhaps, he would take a guided tour with Encarna, and perhaps a coffee afterwards if she was as immune to gossip as she had sounded. He smiled at the thought and walked back to his car.

Next stop Juanma's land. He drove out of the village onto the main road and looked out for a fallow field beyond a mature olive grove. There it was, recently ploughed and with hardly a weed in sight. He pulled over but stayed in the car. It was a large field and should be easily big enough to get permission to build upon, but he would have to ask Salva to check up on that, and also about access to water and electricity. He wouldn't help to sell a field that couldn't be legally built on like some estate agents were said to do. There were many smaller plots around with houses on, his own for one, but you had to twist the council's arm, one way or another, to get a building permit. He would rather stick to houses really, but it was as well to have some land on his portfolio.

"My portfolio," he said as he started the car. "What a laugh!"

It was tricky to find a parking space in Monóvar, so he left his car in the large supermarket carpark on the outskirts and walked in to the bank. He withdrew €10,000 from his main account – two for the house purchase and the rest for wages, windows, doors, tiles and other building supplies that he would soon be buying. He hoped it would be enough and knew that cash was much preferred in the building trade; in any trade for that matter. The bank clerk hadn't batted an eyelid at the amount of cash he had withdrawn – so different from England where he once saw someone paying for a loaf of bread with a bank card.

England, Accrington. It had been a while since he had last visited his sister, he thought as he walked back towards the supermarket with the wad of money firmly zipped into the large inside pocket of his lightweight jacket. Six years? Maybe seven? He ought to pay her a visit, but it wouldn't be till next summer now and only if his venture went well. By next summer he might be on bread and water if the house cost more to do up than he thought and no-one showed any interest in buying it. Still, Marge had an open invitation to visit and it wasn't his fault if his brother-in-law Danny didn't like 'abroad'.

After buying a trolley-load of mostly imperishable goods that would keep him going for a month or two he headed back to the village, thinking about what else he had to do. As was his habit, he decided to get the most irksome things out of the way first, so he parked near Mario's bar with the intention of getting the key to Pablo's house.

"So when do you start?" Mario asked before the door has closed behind him.

"Soon, I hope," Jack replied, eyeing the three men who sat up at the bar. "Have you got a key for me?" he asked as he approached the bar, lifting a finger to his lips.

"Ah, yes," Mario said, reaching under the bar. "What can I get you?" he asked as he handed over the key.

"Nothing just now. I'll be back later."

As he walked down the street he wondered if Mario would respect the confidentiality of their 'clients'. He'd better if he wanted to get his cut. By the time he'd looked at Pablo's house and called María Jesús it would be going up for three and the bar ought to be empty, as very few people availed themselves of the joys of Mario's kitchen. It wasn't that his wife Luisa's cooking was bad, but Julio's *menu del día* was such good value that they found it impossible to compete. He would return the key then and be able to discuss the properties with no eavesdroppers present.

Grumpy Pablo's house was a mess. The window frames were crumbling away, the front door was rotten, and the roof needed replacing. He saw no point in going inside and wasn't sure it was even safe to do so. It was a huge job, and Pablo wasn't asking much less than the price María Jesús had mentioned. He called her and she agreed to meet him at the house on the northern edge of the village. She was a plump, pleasant woman dressed in black and she looked up and down the street before ushering him inside and closing the door behind them. The two-storey house was in a similar condition to the one he was buying from Josemi, only larger, and the €30,000 she was asking made him stop and think.

"You mentioned that Marta charges a percentage. Do you know what percentage?"

"Oh, two or three, I think they said."

"In that case my fee of €1000 isn't very cheap, is it?"

"Isn't it? I'm not very good with percentages. We didn't do them when I was at school," she said with a titter.

"I think I'd only charge you, er… six hundred," he said, remembering Mario's share.

"Listen, Jack, if you get more than thirty, you can keep the rest. I'll be glad to get it off my hands."

"No," he said firmly. "That wouldn't be right. I'll get as much as I can, but all I'm doing is finding a buyer."

"Suit yourself, but I don't begrudge you a thousand. So, what do you think of it?"

"I think you're asking a fair price. It needs some work, but the patio is big and faces south, which the foreigners will like as they enjoy sunning themselves. I'll let you know when anyone wants to see it and we can meet up."

"No, you keep the key for now. Try to show it to people when it's quiet, and don't mention the price to anyone from here. They'll think I'm desperate for money." She laughed and handed him the large door key.

"It might take some time, María Jesús," he said, remembering that he didn't have a single prospective buyer.

"I'll give you a year, ha ha," she said before opening the door and scuttling away down the street.

Jack took another look around the house before locking the door and returning to Mario's.

"So?" Mario asked from his stool behind the empty bar.

"Pablo's asking too much, María Jesús is asking a fair price. Encarna's house looks good from the outside and Juanma's land might sell at that price if he gets permission to build and water and electricity isn't too expensive to connect."

"You sound like an expert already. I think there's water to Juanma's land already, but wouldn't it be up to the buyer to get building permission?"

"Not if I'm selling it. What if they buy and then can't build? What if it costs a fortune to get an electricity connection? No, tell Juanma that he has to look into that before I'll sell it."

"OK, boss."

"Fix me a cheese and tomato *bocadillo* and a glass of wine, please. I'm also thinking that €1000 might be a bit much to ask, you know. None of the properties are dear, so it's quite a big percentage really."

"Nonsense," Mario said as he sliced the bread. "People like round numbers and it's not so much."

"If you say so."

"I've heard, I've just heard, that you might be selling your house and moving into the one you've bought when it's finished."

"Who told you that, Mario?" asked Jack, lifting his hand to his brow.

"Oh, just talk, probably second or third hand."

"Well you tell them that I'm not selling to anyone at any price." Jack emptied his wine glass and returned it to Mario.

"I will." He refilled the glass. "That's certainly the best way to get a good price for it."

"Shit, Mario! I'm not selling and that's final."

Mario nodded and handed over the sandwich. "Point taken, Jack. So, have you got any buyers lined up for these houses then?"

"Not exactly. I'm going to see about that when I leave here."

"The Englishwoman's bar, right?"

"Yes. Pam knows all the foreigners."

"But they've all got houses, haven't they?"

"Yes, but it's word of mouth that brings people out here. They feel safer if they know there are more countrymen around."

Jack found himself devouring his food in order to get out of the bar. He'd left the least annoying task until last, because he liked Pam, but he still wanted to get it over with and return to the peace of his house.

"When do you start on Josemi's house?" asked Mario, sensing that he would soon have no-one to question until coffee time.

"You've already asked that. When it's mine. Soon, I hope."

"Josemi told me about his new job with his cousin. He thinks you're great. He thinks you've brought him luck."

"I hope I've brought us both luck," Jack said, laying a five euro note on the counter and making for the door before

Mario could return it. It wouldn't do to be in this man's debt, especially if he never sold a single house.

As Jack approached Pam's bar he crossed his fingers and willed it to be empty. There was nobody sitting outside and as the three tables were receiving the pleasant afternoon sunshine that is where most of her customers would have chosen to sit. When he pushed the bead curtain aside and saw only Pam's permed grey hair he breathed a sigh of relief. He would have found it almost impossible to say what he had to say had there been anybody there. Touting for any sort of business was hard enough for him even in his Spanish world, but at least there he could pretend he was playacting. However many years you speak a foreign language, it never seems quite as real as your own.

"What can I get you, Jack?"

"Just a coffee, Pam." He glanced around the bar which the fake beams and wooden panels that he and Brian had fitted had helped to give the rustic feel that Pam had desired.

"*Un cortado* para mi amigo, Jack," she said, turning to the machine.

Pam was the only other British person Jack knew here who had made a real effort to learn to speak Spanish correctly and he admired her for it. When she spoke her English accent was still very much in evidence and she had to think for a while before uttering a sentence of any complexity, but she had studied her grammar and meant to use it. Arriving in Spain in her late-fifties had made it more difficult to pick up than it had been for him at thirty-five, but she'd had scores of private classes and still studied a little every day. It was a shame she could hardly ever practise at work.

"Do you know anybody else here who speaks Spanish as well as you do?" he asked, not wanting to plunge straight into house talk after not having had a proper chat with her for weeks.

"Hmm, apart from you, our resident *nativo*, there's Joyce who lives out on the road to Jumilla, and there was Tracy the hairdresser, but she's moved down near Abanilla now. Most of my customers don't show much interest, though I should be glad of that or they might not come here."

"Are new people still coming out to live, or do you think we've had our full quota of Brits?"

"Which question do you want me to answer first?" she asked, chuckling. "No, there are still people who come to look around and they make a beeline for this place, especially when they see my customers sitting outside. I point them to Marta's office next door, if they haven't already been, once they've spent some money."

"Have you never thought about... you know, finding houses for people?" Jack asked, wanting to be sure he wasn't treading on her toes.

"God no, I spend enough hours in here without speaking English in my spare time too. I do a lot of evening classes in Monóvar, you know. I'm on painting at the moment. Look." She pointed to a very watery watercolour in a small frame behind the bar.

"Where did you paint that?"

"From near your house. I walked along that old track that peters out at the top of the rise. It's the best view in the whole area."

They both looked at the view over some indistinct fields to a hazy mountain range.

"Yes, I recognise it," Jack said, nodding.

"Liar, it's awful. It's only on the wall because it was my first attempt."

"You must come for lunch one day and I'll commission you to paint the view from my porch."

"I'll come, and I'll paint it, but there'll be no commission," she said with laughter in her pale blue eyes.

Jack half-expected Pam to ask him if the rumours were true that he was selling his house, but in this Anglo-Saxon outpost he knew that the gossip was akin to that of a hill station in the Indian Empire; completely separate from that of the natives.

"Pam, I wanted to ask your advice about something," he said.

"Spit it out, then. I know you've got something on your mind."

"Well, I'll tell you the whole story some other time, but I'm not working for Brian anymore and I have to find a way to make a little money. My friend Salvador suggested that I might have a go at… selling houses… to the foreigners who come here."

Please don't say, '*You*, Jack?' he thought.

"What a good idea!" she said, a wide smile revealing her fine teeth.

"Do you think so?"

"Of course. You're perfect for it. You speak the language, you know most of the villagers, and you're honest. Who better?"

"Well, I don't exactly have the gift of the gab."

"People don't want to hear bullshit, Jack."

The mild expletive sounded odd coming from someone as motherly as Pam, but he guessed she was right. Just then the bead curtain rustled and two fingers appeared in a victory, or peace, salute.

"That'll be Cliff and Geoff wanting their afternoon pints," Pam said. "Don't worry, they won't come in while there's a ray of sunshine to be had on the street."

She poured the pints in dimpled glasses and took them outside. After a brief exchange she reappeared. "So, Jack, what have you got to sell?"

"Well, so far I've located three, no, two village houses and a plot of land."

"Nothing in the country?"

"Not yet, no, apart from the land."

"A lot of people prefer the country. Those old farmhouses, you know, or something in one of the tiny hamlets, although some do prefer village houses."

"Right, I'll look into it. I plan to charge a flat fee of €1000 for my… services; less if the property is cheap."

"Sounds reasonable, though I wouldn't charge any less. So, how are you going to find buyers, then?"

"Well, I hoped that if you heard of anyone who was looking for a house you could give me a quick ring, you know," Jack said rather sheepishly.

"By which time they're half way to Alicante, or Albacete, or anywhere. No, Jack, what you need are some business cards."

"Business cards? I hadn't thought of that. I'll look into it."

"Look no further, my friend. I didn't do a basic graphic design course at college for nothing. You tell me what you want to put and I'll design them and print a few dozen out."

"Well, thanks, Pam. I'll pay you, of course."

"Ha, you can pay me by coming to see me more often. I haven't forgotten the time when you fixed that leak in my kitchen roof. What shall we put on the cards then?"

"Well. My name, telephone number, and… I don't know, not estate agent, that's for sure. Pour me a small glass of Magno brandy while I think about it, please."

She appeared deep in thought as she poured the drink. "I know, Property Consultant. How does that sound?"

"It sounds a bit… official. I'm just introducing people, after all, and I don't want them to be after me for not paying tax." He chuckled and sipped the brandy. "What about just my name and number? How would that look?"

"Bare. I suppose I could do a sketch of an old house in the background."

"That sounds good. Yes, I think I'd prefer that," he said, conscious of the tax authorities' growing propensity for leaving no stone unturned.

"Well, pop in next week and I'll show you what I've come up with. In the meantime, I'll spread the word and also pounce on any strangers who look like they're after a house. You can spot them a mile off. They look all… dreamy, as if this place were some kind of heaven on earth."

"Well, we like it well enough."

"Yes, I guess we do."

Jack finished his brandy, paid, and stood up to leave. "There's just one more thing, Pam. I have a sort of arrangement with Mario at the bar. If I sell one of the houses that he's told me about, I'll pay him a commission. I'd like to do the same with you if you find me a buyer."

"You and your commissions! You'll end up with nothing. No, I'll be more than glad to help. Would you put them in touch with your friend Salvador regarding the legal work?"

"I'd give them that option, yes."

"That'll be a first, then; two honest people working together on house sales."

"Oh, I imagine Marta is pretty honest from what I know of her," said Jack.

"Have you forgotten who her father is?"

After saying not goodbye but *au revoir* to Pam, Jack set off for home, wishing she hadn't mentioned the baker, albeit indirectly, right at the end of their conversation. He remembered that Marco was another one who was said to covet his enchanted house and hoped that he wouldn't have to rebuff an offer from him too. Mind you, the more rebuffs, the sooner they would get it into their thick heads that he was staying put.

As he began the drive up the last and steepest part of the track he saw the reflection of the afternoon sun on something metallic in front of his house. Perhaps Salva or Vicente had dropped in, he thought, but as he approached the open gate he saw it was a large, blue BMW. He parked his dusty Seat next to it and looked around. Over on the land, between the plum and cherry trees, he saw a slim man gazing down at the valley. Even from a distance of thirty yards his dark, slicked back hair and black glasses, his expensive-looking shirt and trousers, and his now dusty patent leather shoes provoked a feeling of antipathy in Jack, quite apart from the fact that the man hadn't even acknowledged his arrival.

Two can play at that game, he thought, as he hoisted a *bombona* from the boot onto his shoulder and carried it towards the house. As he returned for the second gas bottle the man came over with hand outstretched.

"Hello, I'm Néstor Puig, the lawyer. I hoped to catch you in," he said in the clipped voice of the Spanish *nouveau riche* that Jack had so detested on the phone, but in English today, which sounded even worse. The man looked even more repellent than the voice and reminded him of some business students he had been obliged to teach in Murcia. Conceited and self-satisfied, almost all of them. Jack shook his hand, nevertheless.

"What can I do for you?" he asked, pleased that some flakes of orange paint from the gas bottle had sullied his dainty little hands.

"Do you remember when I phoned you about the house, Jack?"

"I do."

"Well, I'm now in a position to make you a much better offer."

"It's still not for sale."

"You haven't heard the price yet, ha ha ha!"

A loathsome laugh too, more of a cackle really. Jack saw no reason for moving any nearer to the object of Néstor's desires and remained with the *bombona* between them.

"It's not for sale at any price. I wish people would realise that," Jack said calmly. He intended this to be a short, polite and final interview.

"Look at these," Néstor said, fishing two neatly folded sheets of paper from his shirt pocket. "Here you can see four examples of the kind of house you can buy for the money that I'm prepared to offer you."

Short of dropping them on the ground, Jack had little choice but to take the proffered papers and glance at them. There were two glossy photos on each sheet and all four were of attractive houses with pools. Jack returned the sheets without reading the text.

"Or alternatively," went on Néstor, undeterred, "you could buy another small place like this and have a good... nesting egg."

"I've got a good nesting egg, thanks," he said, enjoying the sound of the words. "I've got a nesting egg in the bank and I've just bought an old house as an investment, as I'm sure you know."

"My client is prepared to offer you two hundred thousand for the house and land. He will pay up to half in cash if you prefer."

"I don't normally keep so much money around the house," Jack said in a deadpan voice. "Nesting eggs are better in the bank, preferably a reliable one."

"As you wish. So, what do you say?"

"Well, I'm surprised." Jack beamed at Néstor.

"Yes, it's a fantastic price," he said, beaming back.

"I didn't know the old fatty had so much money."

"Fatty? Oh, Les. No, Les is not my client."

"Oh, who is it?"

"Well, I suppose you'd call them international investors."

Jack looked down into the valley and nodded.

"So, shall I begin to draw up the contract, Jack?"

"What contract?" he asked, looking puzzled.

"For the sale, of course."

"I've already told you it's not for sale."

"But for that price! It's madness not to sell," Néstor said, struggling unsuccessfully to hide his exasperation.

"The house is priceless to me."

"Everybody has their price, Jack, even a stubb-... strong man like you."

"Yes, I suppose I do."

"What?"

"Oh, add a nought onto what you've offered and I'll give it some thought," Jack said before pursing his lips, nodding sagely, and trying hard not to laugh.

"You are trying to ridicule me," Néstor said, his voice more precise than ever. "It is not advisable to ridicule me, Jack."

Jack gazed into the young man's blazing eyes. "Off you go now," he said quietly.

Néstor turned on his heels and stomped over to his car. When he had slammed the door he shot Jack a final wrathful glance. Jack held up his index finger and Néstor lowered the window.

"One more thing, Néstor."

"What?"

"It's nest egg, not nesting egg. Can't have you making a fool of yourself, can we?"

Néstor started the car and powered away, wheels spinning. Jack watched the trail of dust descending the hill and sighed. "Good riddance to bad rubbish," he said aloud, just like his mother used to.

15

Jack woke up on Saturday morning thinking about Néstor, not the most auspicious start to the day, he reflected as he pulled on his shorts. Perhaps it was wrong of him to have treated him badly, but he chuckled when he remembered the look of frustration on the man's face as he drove away. He had seen anger there too, but how did he expect to be rewarded for what almost amounted to harassment? Perhaps he'll have realised once and for all that there's nothing doing and will turn his attention to some other foolish scheme. There must be a hundred views as good or better than his within driving distance that Néstor's 'international investors' could snap up without such fuss and expense.

Two hundred thousand euros though, that *would* produce a nice little nest egg if he bought another similar house. Another ten years of life in Spain if it came to that, if not more. It was tempting, in an abstract sort of way, but when he imagined the entire valley full of luxury chalets, pools and acres of grass and gravel instead of the agriculture that had been around since the Moors were here, and probably before that, he shook his head and put the idea out of his mind.

When his phone rang he thought that one good thing about these mobile devices was that you could see who was calling. He had bought his first mobile phone in about 2005, on

Vicente insisting that he shouldn't be so isolated, and had been much happier about having it once he had learnt how to store people's names. This time it was Josemi, so he pressed the green button.

"Hola, Jack. How's it going?"

"I'm fine. You sound happy this morning."

"Well, it's a nice day. When are we starting on the house?"

"As soon as the sale goes through, which should be on Wednesday. That's when we're seeing the notary, isn't it?"

"Yes, but why not start on Monday? The sooner we start, the more chance there is of finishing before I start working for my cousin."

"That's true," Jack said. "Listen, I'm expecting a call from my sister in England. Can I call you back in half an hour?"

"Sure, Jack"

Another little fib, but the more you interact with people, the more you have to use them, Jack thought as he placed the phone on the table and sat down to think. He hadn't intended to be in any great hurry about finishing the house and he hadn't intended to give Josemi more than two days' work a week, but what difference did it really make? A couple of thousand euros here or there wouldn't make much difference and the sooner the house was ready, the sooner he could employ his hitherto untested selling skills and hand it over to the pleasant retired couple who he envisaged living there. Then again, Salva had suggested hanging on to it for a couple of years until prices rose. Maybe he could rent it out in the meantime, because some expats liked to try out a place before they committed themselves.

What the heck, if Josemi wants or needs the work, why fuss about a bit of money? He made a cup of tea and some toast and rang back when the half hour had elapsed.

"How's your sister?" Josemi asked.

"Oh, she didn't ring. She'll ring later, I suppose. I'm all right to start on Monday if you are. How are you for tools? I don't think I've enough for both of us."

"I've got plenty. I suppose you'll want to get the electrician and plumber in to take a look first."

"Yes, and have someone look at the roof too."

"It's sound, apart from a few cracked tiles at the back. I'll replace those in no time."

"That's good," said Jack, whose head for heights wasn't the best. Brian had always done most of ladder work.

"If you want I'll get Federico to look at the plumbing and old Alfredo to check the wiring," said Josemi.

"Yes, please do. I know them both. I'll need to order new windows and doors too."

"Amadeo's the man to talk to. He's based in Jumilla and prices are always a bit cheaper in Murcia. He sells good products."

"OK, we can get a quote from him. Do you not feel a bit… strange about helping me do up the house where you were born?"

"No, because if you weren't buying it, it'd have gone to the fat *inglés* or some other greedy bastard. Anyway, you never know, you might end up living there yourself."

Jack's gaze drifted from the hills to the fields and down to his rather knobbly old feet. "You never know. Stranger things have happened."

"So, shall we meet at the house on Monday at eight? I'll give you a key."

"Eight's fine. I'll see you then."

The rest of Jack's weekend was relaxing and educational. He finished the Thesiger book and had enjoyed reading about his years with the nomads of Arabia. The nomadic lifestyle had its beauty, but it was a shame that the few nomads who were left only had deserts and steppes to wander over. Soon there would be no nomads or uncontacted tribes left in the world. Change and decay, he thought, but at least he wouldn't let them change this valley, not in his lifetime.

On Sunday evening he had just started a Graham Greene novel about a comical spy in Havana when the phone rang. It was Brian, so he answered.

"Hello, Brian."

"Hi, Jack."

"Everything OK?"

"Not bad. Will you be starting work on that old house you bought soon?"

"Yes, tomorrow morning, in fact."

"I… well, I wondered if there might be any work for me there."

Jack grimaced and held the phone at arm's length for a moment. He exhaled slowly and put it back to his ear. "Well, the trouble is, Brian, that I've promised Josemi, the bloke I bought it from, that I'd give him two or three days work a week on it. There's nothing really major to do and I have to keep costs down."

"Right, well, I just thought I'd ask."

"Is anything wrong, Brian?" he asked, because he sensed that more was amiss than a temporary lack of work. Brian didn't answer right away and Jack could tell that he had stepped outside the house.

"The truth is that Liz is threatening to go back to England."

"For a break?"

"For good, at least that's what she says. To be honest, because I thought Les would be buying that house and I'd be doing it up I haven't been looking very hard for work. I started driving round last week and it turns out that bloody Martínez has picked up at least two good jobs from Brits in the area. Him and his damn business cards," he added bitterly.

"When they see how shoddy his work is, word will soon get round."

"Yes, but that'll take time."

"I... well," began Jack, Brian's acquiescence to Les's ruse to force him to sell his house passing through his mind, "I can't really give you anything, unless Josemi backs out. I've stretched myself to the limit to buy that house, you see, and I just haven't got the cash," he said, feeling that a whitish lie was the best way to extricate himself. "I'll let you know if I hear of any work."

"OK, Jack. I just thought I'd ask. Bye."

Brian had hung up before Jack had been able to express polite concern regarding his wife's intentions, but he was rather glad he had. Over the last few years, whenever he wondered if he might be happier with a woman by his side he thought of Liz and resolved to soldier on alone. Liz was an extreme example, of course, but the truth was that when he thought about *any* of his friends' and acquaintances' wives he treasured all the more keenly his bachelor status. Not that some of them weren't pleasant, but he just couldn't see himself with any of them or anyone like them.

Perhaps he was past it, but as he still had the phone in his hand he decided to ring Encarna anyway. It was only a business call, after all.

"Hola, Encarna. It's Jack, the cycling *guiri*."

"Ha! I was hoping you'd call. Have you found plenty of houses to sell?

"Only two, maybe three, and some land, but your house looks the most promising. I had a look at it the other day. It seems to be in good condition."

"It's not bad. It'll need repainting throughout as during her last years my mother wouldn't have anybody but family in the house."

"Oh," said Jack, injecting as much empathy as he could into the only word he could think of to say.

"So, when shall we meet, Jack?"

"How about tomorrow?"

"That's fine. I'll be back from work at about half past three, but I'd prefer to meet later on, sometime after six."

Jack was about to ask her where she worked and what she did, but refrained. "OK, I might be a bit scruffy as I'll have been seeing to the work on the house that I've bought."

"Don't worry, it's not a date, after all," she said, chuckling.

"Ha ha, no." Jack felt his face going red and was glad she couldn't see him.

"That house is Esperanza's husband's, isn't it?"

"Yes."

"You can't avoid gossip in this place. I mentioned you to a couple of friends and now know your life story; their version of it, anyway. Are you going to be living in the house?"

"No, it's just a… an investment," he said. The word, *inversión*, sounded strange on his lips. It sounded strange full stop, in fact. He hoped she wouldn't allude to the widely held belief that he would soon be dispensing with his main residence.

"It's a nice row of houses," she said. "They're bigger than they look, aren't they?"

"Yes, I'm looking forward to doing it up, with Josemi's help."

"That's good. Being out of work doesn't suit that man. What time shall I expect you then?"

"Six o'clock? Or later?"

"Seven would be better. I'll make sure I'm round at the house by then. Just knock."

"I will. See you, Encarna."

"Ciao, Jack."

Jack hung up and said, "Ciao, Encarna." It sounded a bit too chic for him to say. Perhaps she was a sophisticated lady. Perhaps she loved fashion and other expensive things, or perhaps she read books, or both.

"Perhaps, perhaps, Negro" he said to the cat which he had finally baptised. "I'll knock on the door tomorrow and a great fat lump will open it."

Negro looked up from the chair.

"She'll have a limp too, or just the one leg. Or one eye, in the middle of her forehead."

Tiring of his conversation, Negro slinked between his legs and leap over the porch wall.

"Nonsense, I know. Tomorrow we'll see."

16

The next day Jack drove into the village to meet Josemi at eight and by half past ten Federico the plumber and Alfredo the electrician had already carried out their rather brief inspections. Federico suggested replacing the old gas water heater and re-plumbing just the bathroom, while Alfredo said that the trouble with being such a good worker was that he never got called back to do repairs.

"It must be twenty years since I rewired this place," he said, his cigarette twitching in the corner of his mouth as he spoke. "And I'll be retired before it needs doing again."

Jack guessed that Alfredo was about his own age, but the skinny man's chain smoking and thrice-daily visits to Mario's bar made him look much older. Jack doubted that his retirement would be a long one unless he came across him sometime soon in the bar drinking alcohol-free beer and sucking on a plastic or electronic cigarette like a few of the more mature customers did. The two men left, Federico to return the following week, and Jack invited Josemi to an *almuerzo* at Mario's.

"Thanks, but I'd prefer not to go to Mario's. He'd hide under the table to hear what we were saying if he had to."

"I doubt he'd fit. Perhaps he'll get the place wired with mics one day. Julio's then?"

"Hmm, how about the bar of the *inglesa*?"

"Pam's? Yes, if you want. Her *bocadillos* are just as good as Julio's. Have you been there before?"

"No, but I fancy a change. Perhaps I'll pick up a bit of English."

"Ha, you might."

The two men walked down to the bar and Josemi headed through to the bathroom.

"Hi, Pam," said Jack. "That's Josemi, the bloke I bought the house from."

"Nice to see a Spaniard in here. I've got something to show you." She leant down and produced a large sheet of paper. "It's just an idea. What do you think?"

Jack looked at the business card-sized sketch of a house very much like his own. His name was printed just above the roof and his telephone number appeared to be painted on the porch wall.

"It's really good, Pam. Discrete, just the job. Will you have to send it away for printing, because-"

"No no no! I have plenty of card and a little guillotine, so if you like it I'll print out fifty or so."

"Thanks, but I must pay-"

"Order something and shut up," she said. "Besides, you bringing your friend here might start a new trend."

Jack looked at the sketch again and folded the sheet. "The cards will remind me what I'm doing all this for. I'll not show it to my pal yet," he said, handing back the sheet as Josemi returned. He introduced him to Pam.

"Hola, Josemi. Pleased to meet you. What can I get you both?"

They order their *bocadillos* and red wine with lemonade and continued chatting in Spanish. When a Scotsman approached the bar she passed the time of day with him, before addressing Josemi again.

"Are you going to teach this old *inglés* a few tricks about building then?"

"Oh, there might be one or two things." He smiled and looked round the bar. "Nice place."

"Yes, Jack here did most of the woodwork; him and Brian." At the mention of his ex-employer Pam saw Jack's face drop. She would ask him why some other time, but there was another person who she decided to tell him about. "Les was in here yesterday," she said in Spanish. "He sat in that corner over there on his own and drank five pints of beer one after the other, looking more and more depressed. Then he paid and left without a word. Drove home, I suppose."

"Strange," said Jack. "Sounds like he's feeling low."

"It's what he deserves," said Josemi. "Has he contacted you about your house, Jack?"

The question surprised Jack, as he hadn't filled him in on all the details of his tribulations, but he guessed that Josemi heard as much gossip as everybody else.

"No, not for a while. Perhaps he's changed his plans. Better for all concerned if he has, especially him."

Jack sipped his wine while Pam and Josemi chatted about some mutual acquaintances. If Les had given up on the idea of buying his house it would be one less pest to worry about. He had heard nothing from Martínez recently and nothing at all from the other alleged pretender, Marco the baker. Maybe it was just Néstor and his investors now. Sounded like a pop group.

"A penny for your thoughts, Jack." Pam said in English, before trying a very literal translation on Josemi. '*Un penique para tus pensamientos,*' left him nonplussed, so she told him what she had meant. They both looked at Jack.

"Oh, I was just thinking about Les and the whole house business," Jack said in Spanish. "Perhaps they're going to leave me alone, after all."

"When they see your cards they'll know you're not for moving," said Pam.

When they returned to the house at twelve, Amadeo, the window and door man from Jumilla, was waiting for them. He handed Jack a brochure and went off to inspect the house. On his return Jack asked him how much the wood-coloured PVC windows would cost and received a scribbled quote within the minute. The price was lower than expected, so he asked about a full set of doors. After producing another brochure and taking another tour round, Amadeo, a compact, taciturn man of forty, told him the prices.

"That's for cash, of course," he added.

"Of course. I'll have some doors and doorframes too then."

"Keep the brochure, make your choice, and let me know next week when I come to fit the windows."

"I will, but Josemi and I were going to fit the windows, and the doors too."

"Fitting is included in the price. My men will fit them."

"That's great, Amadeo."

"I told you he was your man," said Josemi.

"And even cheaper than usual because Josemi here refused his little commission. Josemi, you are turning into a saint.

Adiós to you both." He turned and left before they could raise their hands above waist level.

"He doesn't waste time, does he?" said Jack.

"He's a phenomenon. He has a big warehouse and loads of work all over the place. It just shows that some people are still doing well in Spain."

"Like you will be when your cousin sees what you're capable of. Shall we pull up a few floor tiles before lunch?"

"Yes, we can do the small bedroom in that time. Do you want to save the tiles?"

"Not really."

"Then we can do two bedrooms. I'll get the hammers and chisels."

When they sat down to lunch at Josemi and Esperanza's house – Josemi had insisted – they had removed the tiles from two and half rooms, Josemi having done about two-thirds of the work.

"This stew is excellent, Esperanza. Your cooking obviously keeps your man strong. He made me feel like an old weakling this morning."

"I've been resting up for almost two years," Josemi said. "God, it feels good to work again."

Esperanza smiled at her husband and Jack thought she looked prettier and more radiant than the last time he saw her. He too had enjoyed the hearty tile clobbering session and was pleased that his back was none the worse for wear. He marvelled at how quickly things were moving. At this rate they would be done within a month and he would be looking for a buyer, or better still, someone to rent. He had never seen himself as a member of the capitalist class, but there was no denying the fact that a modest monthly income would do him no harm at all.

An hour later they returned to the house and saw the skip that Josemi had ordered outside the front door.

"That will be full in no time," said Josemi, rubbing his hands together and showing no signs of post-lunch lethargy. "Let's get those tiles up and then we can start removing the inner doors."

By ten past six there were only two tiled rooms left in the house and Jack suggested knocking off for the day. He decided to tell Josemi why.

"I'm meeting someone about a house at seven, so I'd better nip home for a shower. I've decided to try to make some money by bringing buyers and sellers together. My pension prospects are very poor, you see, and I'll have to keep earning money for some time yet."

"And this one? Did you say it would be for some relatives of yours?"

"That was a *mentira piadosa*, I'm afraid." While Jack waited for Josemi's reaction he thought that 'pious lie' made slightly more sense than white lie, but not much.

"I guessed it was, but no matter," said Josemi, nodding pensively.

"No, but this house already feels quite special to me. I shall make sure that whoever buys it are nice folk. I might even try to rent it out. What do you think about foreigners coming to the village, Josemi?"

"Me? I think it's good. They buy and restore the houses that we no longer want and so far have all been tranquil people. They spend money and add a little... colour."

"Yes, mostly red. Do most people think like you do?"

"Most people, yes. A few complain that they'll make house prices rise, but the young people here want new houses and the council ensures that the prices of those are regulated."

Jack thought about the cracks in the houses on Josemi and Esperanza's row, but made no comment. Perhaps now that his new friend was feeling re-energised he would do something about the ones on his house walls. They were certainly a monument to Martínez's incompetence and might explain why he now worked mostly outside the village.

"Well, I don't know if I'll manage to sell many houses, or even this one, but I shan't sell to anyone who would be bad for the village."

"Oh, don't worry. Older *guiris* behave well, apart from Les, and we don't have to see his fat face very often. Here's a key to the front door. I'll stay for a while and throw all the old tiles into the skip."

"Do you want me to pay you every day, or every week?"

"Every week is fine, but today has only been five hours of work."

"No, no," Jack protested. "You've seen to so many other things too."

"I can also do favours for my friends, Jack," said Josemi, touching him lightly on the chest. "Now off you go or you'll be late. Who are you seeing?"

"A lady called Encarna. The house belonged to her mother. It's near Ramón's."

"A nice woman. You'll like her."

As Jack drove home to shower and change he wondered if Josemi's final look had been a knowing one. No matter, in half an hour he would be face to face with the woman he had been thinking about on and off all day.

Dressed in trousers for only the second time since the spring, Jack knocked on the door at exactly seven o'clock.

"That's what I call *puntualidad británica*," said the slender, attractive lady who opened it a few seconds later. "Come in and I'll show you round."

Jack was disappointed. She was probably fifty, but looked a little younger, and her brown eyes were lively and intelligent. Her shoulder-length hair was dark with just a few wisps of grey. Her trousers and sweater were simple but stylish. She had a spring in her step and Jack guessed that she kept herself fit. From behind she could have passed for thirty. He would have no chance, even if she hadn't been wearing a wedding ring.

"Like I said, it will need repainting, but with all this old furniture removed it shouldn't look too bad," she said in her singsong voice after they had toured the ground floor. She even *sounded* too young for him.

"I think you're right. With a coat of paint I think people will see its potential," he said, appearing to find the house fascinating.

"I'll get my sons to move most of the furniture into one room when they come home next weekend."

"What do they do, your sons?"

"They're both studying. Andrés in Alicante and Eduardo in Madrid."

Both studying, probably in their early twenties. Which makes her, what? Jack thought as she led him up the stairs.

"It's my birthday, you see, so they're both coming home to see their old mum." She laughed and opened the bathroom door. "It's not too bad, is it? It was redone about ten years ago."

"It looks fine, and the kitchen is fine too. I think you should ask a bit more for the house."

"Whatever you say, Jack. You're the expert, after all."

"Ha, I'm no expert, I'm afraid, but a friend said I should have a try at selling them."

"Was that Salvador?"

"Yes," Jack said, surprised.

"I know Chelo, you see, and asked her about you."

"Right," he said, fearing the worst.

"She told me you were a great reader. I love reading too, mainly Spanish literature, so I was especially keen to meet you."

Jack felt that his chances had gone from zero to... slightly above zero, but that wedding ring was still an impregnable barrier. A married woman flirting with him? It didn't feel like that, somehow.

"Right, well, when I find someone who might be interested in the house, I'll give you a call," he said, taking a step towards the stairs.

"You're not rushing off already, are you? I thought we might have a drink at Julio's." She looked into his eyes and saw the uneasiness that her words had produced. "Don't worry about this, by the way." She pointed to the only ring on her left hand. "This is my way of saying, 'leave me alone' to the village men and the ones I see at work." She laughed. "I was divorced seven years ago. My ex lives in Villena now. He's a teacher."

"Where do you work?" Jack felt brave enough to ask.

"In Yecla, for the town council. I'm an administrator."

"Is it interesting work?"

"Not especially, but one is glad to be a *funcionaria* in times like these. It's a job for life, after all. How about that drink then?"

"Do you fancy trying the new restaurant? I'll buy you dinner if you like."

"All right then. I haven't been there yet."

When they entered the dimly-lit restaurant near the main road it was evident that few other villagers had become patrons either. The colourful signs the owner had erected on the road attracted a few lunchtime passers-by who didn't know of Julio's bar, but in the evenings it was said to be dead. Tonight there was the optimistic young owner from Valencia, an elderly foreign couple, and themselves, besides a cook presumably standing by in the kitchen. Jack liked the atmosphere, or lack of it, and felt more relaxed than he would have done in Julio's. He was the subject of enough gossip as it was without walking in there with Encarna.

She chose a light dinner of salad followed by fish and he ordered the same. He asked for a bottle of their best white wine to make up for their frugality and felt lost for words as they waited for it to arrive. He looked around the simply decorated dining room and hoped that Encarna would break the ice.

"Pretend we're still chatting in the house, Jack," she said, touching his forearm across the table and smiling.

"Oh, yes, I don't dine out very often. I've got out of the habit, I'm afraid."

"This is more like dining in, there are so few people here," she said, glancing across at the old couple who were concentrating on their steaks.

The owner's checked shirt was obscured by a white chef's jacket when he reappeared with the wine in an ice bucket, so at least he wasn't paying staff to sit around. Jack mentioned this to Encarna whilst pouring the wine.

"Yes, but he won't last long if things don't pick up. When I drive past after work there are never many cars outside. Perhaps you could bring your clients here when they come to view your houses."

"Ha, I haven't got any yet, though I've only just started."

"I can spread the word in Yecla, if you like. Do you have any leaflets or anything?"

"A friend is making some business cards for me, but they'll only have my name and number on."

"Ha, very discrete, Jack. Just like you, I guess."

"Perhaps I'll ask my friend Pam to make me some leaflets too then. Another friend who works as a policeman in Monóvar offered to put some up there."

"That'll be Vicente. I went to school with him."

Jack sipped his wine and nodded. Vicente had turned fifty-five earlier in the year. "Oh, were you in the same class?"

"No, he's five or six years older than me."

"Ah."

"You're wondering how old I am. Forty-nine this weekend. You could just have asked, you know."

Jack waited for the blood to rush to his face, but for some reason it didn't. He felt increasingly at ease with this charming lady and finished his wine in the hope that it would loosen his tongue. Once the owner-chef had brought their salads and a basket of bread he began, with a little prompting, to tell her about how he had ended up living near the village.

"So, you were seeking peace and solitude and you found it," she said.

"Until a few weeks ago, yes. Since then things have not gone so smoothly." After a pause to allow the young *Valenciano* to replace the salad plates with their main dish, he told her about his money worries, his endeavours to come up with a solution to them, and the apparent conspiracy to remove him from his house.

"Good heavens, if someone else were telling me this I wouldn't believe them. Les sounds awful and Néstor *is* awful. A cousin of mine went out with him for a while; a short while. It's strange because the rest of the family are nice people."

"Perhaps that's what city life, and ambition, can do to a person," said Jack, removing the fish bones with his knife as his mother had taught him to do. "What's Yecla like?" he asked, feeling they had spent enough time on him and his problems.

"Oh, it's no city, but it's a busy town. I normally come straight home from work, but there's a good theatre and I sometimes go to the plays there. They get some of the top Spanish actors. I watched *En el Estanque Dorado* there a few months ago."

"On Golden Pond? I've seen the film. I'd like to visit the theatre sometime. I should read more Spanish books too, but hardly ever seem to get round to it. Spanish fiction is a bit… florid for me, or maybe just too difficult."

"Have you tried Pío Baroja?"

"I've heard of him but never read anything of his."

"He has a very clear style and he's very good. I'll lend you a couple of his books."

For the next hour they chatted away about books, authors, places they had visited, and local walks. Encarna was a keen walker, which explained her trim figure, and offered to show him a good route in the hills to the north of the village.

"We could go the Saturday or Sunday after next," she said as she stirred her coffee. "Unless you're too tired after working on the house."

"Oh, I doubt it. It looks like Josemi has got energy enough for the two of us." He told her about their day's labours and how he expected to finish the house within a few weeks.

"Then get some leaflets printed and I'll leave some in and around the town hall in Yecla. Remember you have to sell my house too."

"And for a good price. I can see an older couple buying it, you know. People who want amenities nearby.

"You might want to live in the village when you're older too, for the same reason."

"Maybe, but it'll be a while yet, I hope. I'm sixty you know."

"I know, but you look younger. You seem younger too when you relax. Come on, walk me home. I have to be up at six."

Jack was relieved when she didn't dispute his right to pay the bill, though she said it would be her turn next time, and even more relieved when she offered him her cheek after unlocking the door of her modern two-storey house which was too stylish to be Martínez-built. Maybe they'd kiss just once next time, on the lips, he thought as he walked back to the car feeling rather lightheaded, or maybe they wouldn't. Either way he felt extremely happy to have met her. She liked him too, he knew.

"Time will tell, old boy," he said to himself in the rear-view mirror.

It took him a long time to get to sleep that night.

17

On Tuesday morning Josemi finished annihilating the floor tiles while Jack carried the fragments to the skip outside. They ate *almuerzo* at Pam's, on Jack, and lunch at Josemi's, courtesy of Esperanza, and decided that this was the best arrangement.

"The good thing about Pam's is that you don't get the gossip-mongers annoying you all the time like in the other bars," said Josemi as they walked back to the house after lunch, he with a huge hammer-drill over his shoulder.

"Oh, I think her customers are probably gossips too; they just can't understand what we're talking about," said Jack, feeling happier than he had for a long time. His phone stayed switched on now, in case Encarna called him or sent him one of those text messages that he had never got round to using. The pack of business cards in his pocket made him feel good too and Pam had agreed to make him a simple leaflet which he would get copied at Reme's burgeoning establishment.

In the afternoon they took turns at operating the heavy drill to remove the old plaster and transporting the debris to the rapidly filling skip. They knocked off at seven and Jack suggested a drink at Mario's. The two dusty men found a place at the busy bar and Jack ordered bottles of beer. They were the object of polite curiosity to the other patrons, who couldn't help but see that the two men got on well, despite their unusual working arrangement. Mario's face was twitching oddly, which led Jack to believe that he wished to speak to them alone. Jack led Josemi to a corner table and, sure enough, Mario was there like a shot.

"Well?" he asked, as if more exact questioning were unnecessary.

"Well what?" asked Jack after taking a long drink from his bottle.

"How is the work going? Have you seen all the houses I told you about? Have you found any buyers?" he rattled off in a hoarse whisper.

"Oh, only that? Bring us two more beers and some crisps and olives and I'll tell you."

After one more sip of beer Mario was back with three bottles and after a second the crisps and olives were on the table and Mario on a chair.

"You move fast when you want to," said Josemi, laughing.

"Well, Mario, to answer your questions one by one. The work is going extremely well and much faster than I believed possible. We've done twice as much as Brian and I would have managed, thanks to this young man's tremendous staying power." He waited for Mario to file that snippet of information away for future use. "Of the houses you informed me of, I think Encarna's and María Jesus's are the best bets. Encarna will have hers ready for painting soon.

Pablo will have to reduce his price substantially for me to even attempt to sell that old ruin. Juanma's land depends on him sorting out the things I mentioned, but I'll show it to prospective customers. Have any more properties come up yet?"

"Not yet, but they will. I'm working on it," Mario said, tapping the side of his nose.

"Good, because Pa-, because an English friend has suggested that what most *ingleses* prefer are houses in the country or in small *aldeas*. If you could find me one or two of those it should be possible to sell them quickly," Jack said with a self-assurance that seemed to surprise no-one but himself.

"Have you not seen Juan's house yet?"

"Er, no. I called him twice but he didn't answer."

"*Caramba*! The house he is selling is perfect. It's one of a group of five or six houses some way off the road to Monóvar. You take the track on the left about four kilometres from the village."

"I know the place. Tell him to answer his phone. I'll give you a few of these," Jack said, handing him a dozen business cards. "I'll have some leaflets ready soon… when they return from the printers," he added, winking at Josemi while Mario studied the cards.

"Hmm, I hope the leaflets will carry more information than these cards, Jack."

"They will explain clearly what I do and will contain my number but not my name. I don't want to attract the attention of *Hacienda*, do I?"

"Ah, no," Mario said with a knowing leer, inveterate tax dodger that he was. "Have there been any further developments with… you know what?" he said, casting a sidelong glance at Josemi.

"What?" Jack asked. It was fun to tease Mario today.

Mario glanced at Josemi again and raised his eyebrows at Jack. "Other property matters, or perhaps you cannot speak now."

"I have no secrets from my partner. To cut a long story short, I've had a generous offer from Néstor on behalf of some undisclosed investors, which I rejected, but no further annoyance from Les, Martínez or anybody else."

Mario tried to hide his disappointment by taking a long drink of beer.

"I thought you were abstaining from alcohol this month, Mario," said Jack.

"I managed almost two weeks, but my body began to cry out for nourishment."

"You need to exercise. Come to work on the house when it's quiet here. It's doing me a world of good," Josemi said, punching his chest lightly.

Mario studied Josemi's face for a moment. "Who would have thought that things would work out so well, eh, Josemi?"

"And they will only get better."

* * *

The following day Jack picked up Josemi and Salvador and they drove to the notary's office in Monóvar. They concluded the business quickly and the notary – a solemn man as notaries usually are, or pretend to be – had no need to step outside for a moment on some flimsy pretext because Jack had given Josemi the two thousand in cash the day before.

"How do you feel about the sale now that it's done?" Jack asked him on the trip back.

"I feel fine. It's all part of a bigger plan now. I need the money to buy the van, which will make me more money in the long run."

"I'm glad you feel that way. It also seems to be having the effect that I desired. They appear to have given up on the idea of buying my house. What do you think, Salva?" he said over his shoulder. "Do you think they've given up?"

"Hmm, it appears so, but Néstor is a tenacious son of a bitch. He will be pressing these mysterious investors to offer you more money."

"That's fine, he can offer as much as he likes. There's nothing else he can do, is there?"

"No, I suppose not. The house insurance is now valid for the new property, by the way."

"Are those two phrases connected in any way, Salva?"

"They weren't meant to be. Perhaps my subconscious fears that Néstor will resort to underhand ways if you don't agree to sell."

"I doubt it. He's got his career to consider."

"Hey, why don't we take a look at the house that Mario mentioned yesterday," said Josemi, pointing to a cluster of old dwellings some way to their right.

"Ah, the one belonging to a certain Juan," Jack said, before pressing the indicator and slowing down.

They followed the narrow, asphalt track through olive groves and parked in a clearing near the shabby settlement. An old man observed them from a chair outside his house. Jack asked him which house belonged to Juan and the man told him it was the end one.

"It'll fall down unless he uses it or sells it," said the old man, appearing to relish the prospect.

"His house doesn't look too sound, either," whispered Josemi after glance up at the roof. "But it should last him out."

The three men stationed themselves a few yards from Juan's large, two-storey house and examined it. The ancient, rotting door was secured by means of a padlock and chain and the windows that weren't broken were grimy with dust behind the rusting bars. Large, irregular stones were visible behind the crumbling cement façade and many of the heavy roof tiles were askew.

"A ruin," said Salva.

"A pity," said Josemi.

"An exciting restoration project; that's what I'll call it," said Jack, patting his two friends on the back.

"Do you think some crazy *guiri* will buy it?" asked Josemi.

"Yes. If the price is right, which I think it is, it will appeal to many of my compatriots." He looked up at the roof. "Some of them, anyway, if they're brave, or wealthy. This is the sort of job that Brian would like. If I manage to sell it I'll put him in touch with the buyers."

"Let's go," said Salva. "Vicente will be waiting for us at the new restaurant where you're forcing us to eat."

"Got to give them a chance," said Jack. "I'm a bit off Julio's at the moment and Mario's would be too… intense."

"Intense?" Salva asked. "Isn't he normally empty at lunchtime?"

"Yes, that's why it, or he, would be intense. Are you up for lunch, Josemi? My treat."

"No, thanks. I'll leave you guys to it."

"Are you sure?" asked Jack as he climbed into the driver's seat.

"Yes, Esperanza wants us to eat with her mother today."

Jack entered the village to drop Josemi off.

"Eight o'clock tomorrow then, Jack?"

"I'll be there, ready for action."

Vicente's small car was parked in the almost empty restaurant car park and they found him seated at the bar, talking to the owner.

"Vicente's the one who should be selling houses," Jack said to Salva as they approached them. "He's the sociable type."

"Yes, be sure to give him some of those leaflets you gave me. If there's anybody within the boundaries of Monóvar who wants one of your properties he will find them."

"*Chicos!* I'm just having a chat with Tomás here. "Tomás, beers for my friends, please."

"It's on me today," said Jack.

"I know. That's why I'm sampling these fine prawns. Don't worry, Tomás, I will point many people in this direction."

"Thanks, Vicente," said the smiling owner.

They took their glasses to the table that Tomás had prepared by the window and sat down. Three more tables were occupied, each by a single man, probably sales reps passing through.

"So, Jack, I believe you've started work on that old house," said Vicente as he looked at the *menú del día* chalked up on a small blackboard near the entrance.

"Yes, Josemi and I have started with a vengeance, especially Josemi. He's a great worker. What do you think of these?" he asked, producing a folder from which he extracted a leaflet. He had printed two hundred that morning, two to a page, and Reme had cut them with her guillotine.

"Hmm, a nice sketch of your house in the background. Why is the English writing twice as big as the Spanish?"

"Because the *ingleses* are twice as likely to buy the houses."

"More than that," said Salva. "The properties you have mentioned will appeal to very few Spaniards."

"I know, but it seemed rude not to put it in Spanish too. What do you think of the text, Vicente?"

"Hmm, *rural and village houses for sale... plots of land in the country with permission for building... single €1000 fee... legal advice available...* That last bit will be this rogue, I suppose."

"It is."

"Yes, it's a good leaflet. Simple and clear. Give me a hundred."

"A hundred?"

"Yes, I'll ask for more when I need them. Monóvar is quite big, you know. I know a lot of people and there are many lampposts."

"Won't you get in trouble, for... dereliction of duty or something?"

"Ha, my duty is to walk around and make sure that everyone and everything is all right. That is what policing is all about, or should be. Like I said the other week, when they force me into the office I will retire, buy a little house in the country, and become self-sufficient."

"You bachelors can do that," said Salva, a trace of envy in his voice.

The food and wine soon arrived and Vicente entertained them with tales of his dancing exploits. Over coffee and brandy Salva told them about his steadily increasing workload.

"Things are undoubtedly improving," he said. "Past frauds and failures are being slowly forgotten and there's an increasing willingness to *do* things. Spain has been in a state of shock for a long time and is now waking up. This should be good for your venture, Jack. A colleague told me the other day that the Northern Europeans are now beginning to snap up cheap houses."

"I hope so. If they snap up a couple of the ones I've got it'll take the pressure off. I was going to take my time doing up the old house, but Josemi is keen to work every day – he's going self-employed in November – and we might as well get it finished."

"That house will be the first one you'll want to sell, I suppose," said Vicente.

"No, not at all. I'm starting to feel attached to it. I might rent it out, if I can."

"A wise move," said Salva. "At last you are showing some business sense, Jack."

"And Marco, the demon baker, asked me about your house again the other day," said Vicente, twitching his eyebrows Groucho Marx style.

"And Néstor, the demon lawyer," said Jack in a low voice, "has offered me two hundred thousand for it, on behalf of some unknown party."

"Snap it up!" said Vicente, slapping the table. "Your money worries are over."

"No, I'm staying put."

"But it's only a house."

"Yes, *my* house."

* * *

"Hello Denise, it's Liz here."

"Hi, Liz. Just a minute." She stood up and moved her sun lounger out of the encroaching shade. In the early evening it was too cool to sunbathe near the pool, so she had moved onto the more sheltered porch. She lit a cigarette and made herself comfortable. "How are you, love?"

"Oh, not too bad."

"You don't sound very happy."

"No, I'm not really. Brian has practically no work at the moment. You know that scheming bastard Jack has started work on the house that your Les was going to buy, don't you?"

"Les said something about it," she said. She looked over her shoulder to see if her husband had moved. No, he was still on the sofa, staring at the TV, glass in hand.

"Has Les found another old house to do up yet, Denise?"

"Les still has his black dog, I'm afraid."

"His…? Oh, is he still down?"

"In the dumps, yes."

"Like me then. So has he given up on the idea of buying Jack's house and the land in the valley?"

"Not altogether. When he's had just the right amount to drink he sometimes comes round a bit and says that he'll buy the old northern sod out if it's the last thing he does. But with no Néstor and with him hardly ever leaving the house, I can't really say that he's doing anything about it. I told him to go and offer Jack 180 or even 200 thousand and see what he says. If he got Jack's house I think he'd be his old self again."

"Do you think so?"

"Yes, I do. He's like that. Down one minute and up the next, just like Churchill."

Liz had a vague idea who Churchill was and doubted he had much in common with that fat slob. "If Brian doesn't get some work soon, I'm going back to England, for good."

"I don't blame you, dear. The only good thing about this country is the sunshine. I mean, lousy food, ignorant people-"

"I don't *want* to go, especially after all the exciting plans we were talking about the other day, so I'm really hoping that Les will… start feeling better."

Denise stifled a yawn. "Oh, I'm sure he will, dear. It's just a matter of time. Some little thing will happen one day soon and he'll be like Churchill was the day war broke out."

"What was he like?"

"Rampant." Denise looked down at her bulky bosom and sighed. "I'll let you know when there's any news, Liz."

"Please do, Denise. I'm counting on you."

18

When the last of the plaster had been removed from the walls on Thursday afternoon Jack felt that the destruction had ended and the construction was about to begin.

"What shall we do next, Josemi?" he asked as they stood in the dusty shell of a house.

"Now it is time to *enyesar*. The ceilings first of all."

"The plastering, yes. I'm not very good at Spanish-style plastering, or English-style for that matter. The plaster you use here dries very fast and by the time I've got the stuff ready it's already going off."

"I can do the plastering. I'm not a qualified *yesaire*, but I'm quite competent. I'll show you how to mix it how I like it and you can hand me the buckets as fast as I empty them."

"That suits me."

"We'll start the ceilings tomorrow and the walls once the new windows and doors are in next week."

"Until tomorrow morning at eight then," Jack said as he locked the front door.

"I'll be here."

Jack had cycled in that morning and after deciding against another interrogation at Mario's he freewheeled down the road out of the village. On reaching the end of Encarna's street he wondered whether he should call on the pretext of giving her some of the leaflets that he carried in his rucksack, but he decided against it. He would ring her on Monday to wish her a belated happy birthday and invite her to dinner. This pleasant thought occupied him all the way to the foot of the climb up to his house and he had just engaged bottom gear when his phone rang. He stopped, fished the phone from his bag, and was disappointed not to see Encarna's name on the screen.

There was no name on the screen, only a number, but as Vicente might have already begun his papering of Monóvar with the leaflets he thought he'd better answer it. He decided to let the caller speak first.

"Hola, Jack?"

"Hola."

"It's Marco here?"

"Marco? Which Marco?" he asked, though he knew his deep, rather ponderous voice very well.

"The baker. I wanted to ask you a question, Jack. Is your house still for sale?"

"*Still* for sale? It's never been for sale, Marco."

"Oh, I'd heard it was."

"You mustn't believe all the gossip you hear."

"No, of course not. So, I don't suppose you would accept an offer of €150,000 then?"

"How can I accept an offer on something that is not for sale, Marco?"

"Well, I thought that if-"

"Would you sell me your shoes if I asked to buy them?"

"No, well... yes, if the price were high enough."

"OK, then I will offer you ten euros for the shoes you are wearing now."

"I'm wearing sandals," he said, perplexed.

"Real leather?"

"Yes, very good leather."

"Then I'll give you twenty. Please bring them round now." Jack hoped that the somewhat obtuse baker would understand the parable, and the pause which ensued gave him hope.

"I'll sell them for thirty," he said. "Why are you groaning?"

"Because you've missed the point… but you might have touched upon another interesting one. If your sandals were of great sentimental value, how much would you sell them for? A hundred?"

"Not if they were of great sentimental value, no."

"How about a thousand?"

"Then I would have to think about it."

"And do you think I would pay one thousand euros for your sandals?"

"Er, no."

"Well that is the case with my house. I don't mind telling you – and please pass on the information to whoever you wish – that an undisclosed party has offered me two hundred thousand for the house and I turned them down. It is of great sentimental value to me, but for one million euros I would probably sell it. Can you afford that, Marco?"

"Are you mocking me, Jack?" he asked, sounding irate.

"No, no, I'm merely making a point. Look, forget my house, Marco, and find something else to think about. It's really worth little more than a hundred thousand and it's stupid to imagine that it's worth more because of foolish chatter… Marco?"

Marco hanging up on him erased his feeling of pleasantly fatigued wellbeing and instead of the cool shower that he had planned he took up the hoe and began to thrash at the weeds around the cherry trees. Would they ever leave him in peace? Would his interrupted message to Marco be relayed to the relevant parties? Would they throw in the towel or would it stoke the fire of avarice even more? In half an hour his frustration had subsided and he returned to the house. After showering and eating a light dinner he tried to look on the bright side. Marco was the last of the pretenders to contact him and he too had been rebuffed. Perhaps they would now see sense, the lot of them.

"Money is our madness, our vast collective madness," he quoted to the cat, who lay at his feet licking his paws. "Though I don't suppose you've read much Lawrence, have you, Negro?"

* * *

By *almuerzo* time the next day Jack was feeling guilty about his paltry exertions compared to the vast amount of effort that Josemi was putting into the plastering. While ensuring that the young man always had a bucket of the white mixture at hand he marvelled at the speed at which he applied the stuff. It was a warm, sunny September day and Josemi changed his sodden t-shirt before they strolled down to Pam's.

"Our usual *bocadillos* and red wine with a big bottle of lemonade, please, Pam," said Josemi as they sat down at the table nearest to the bar. He rolled his shoulders and stretched his arms. "Just as well it's the weekend tomorrow, Jack. It's hard work when you're not used to it, especially doing the ceilings."

"It looks brutally hard."

"Yes, many *yesaires* are worn out when they reach their fifties. Still, it will help to remove this," he said, patting his paunch.

"You'll be as strong as an ox by the time you start working for your cousin," said Pam as she opened the wine and lemonade bottles. "*That* has already begun to have an effect," she said to Jack, pointing at an enlarged version of the leaflet that she had pinned to the wood clad pillar at the end of the bar.

"Oh, has someone shown interest?"

"Yes, an Irish couple called in yesterday. They'd spent the morning with Marta, viewing houses, and came in to recover from her sales patter in that awful English voice of hers."

"Hmm, it's funny that when she speaks Spanish she sounds fine, but in English she comes across as being almost aggressive. I heard her in the street once," said Jack.

"Anyway, they said they were looking for an old place in the country, but not too far from other houses."

"Would they be interested in some land?"

"I don't think they want to build from scratch. Why? Have you nothing suitable yet?"

"No... unless this Juan answers his phone. He's selling an old house in the little *aldea* on the left as you go towards Monóvar. A very old house, in fact, but I can't get hold of him. I'll try him again later."

"Do that. I've got the couple's number. They thought your fee very reasonable. Now, eat up both of you or you'll never grow."

The rest of the day was tiring but fruitful and they left the house feeling happy with their progress. Josemi had plastered two ceilings, while Jack, as well as mixing many buckets of *yeso*, had finally spoken to the elusive Juan. He turned out to be an amiable old widower who had lived in a small house in the village for the last ten years.

"I like to spend my time with the other *pensionistas*, you see, playing dominos at the social centre," he had told Jack. "Once I retired I knew I would die of boredom out there with just that old grumbler and a few cats for company."

"Does nobody live in the other houses there?"

"No, some go at the weekends and some in the holidays, but he is the only one who lives there all year round."

"Do you think he'd appreciate having a couple of *guiris* for neighbours?"

"Oh, he'll grumble if they don't speak Spanish, but he'll be glad of the company really."

"Right. When I have someone to show the house to, I'll call you again," Jack said, having seen enough of the house to make a viewing of the interior unnecessary.

"Yes, after eight in the evening I am always in. How much did you say you'll get for it?"

"At least twenty-five thousand, plus one thousand for my services. If I get more it's all for you."

"It will be for my grandchildren, as I want for nothing."

Jack paid Josemi for his week's work and was pleased that he preferred to get home to Esperanza than join the other workers in the bars. After calling at Mario's for a quick beer and receiving another number to call, he mounted his bike and headed for home, looking forward to a restful weekend. He would ring the new number and also give the Irish couple a call, but other than that he had no plans.

As he crested the rise and passed between the metal gateposts he sensed that something was amiss. The house looked all right and the front door was closed, but something didn't feel right. He turned to face the land and saw that his few remaining tomato canes were no longer upright. On closer inspection he discovered that they had been pulled out of the ground and one had been broken. Some lettuces lay strewn around and a few branches had been broken from his plum trees. He saw that his car was undamaged and quickly returned to the house and unlocked the door. He checked each room and found splinters of glass on the floor of the spare bedroom to the rear of the house and a large stone just small enough to fit between the window bars lying on the floor. Another tour of the house and land told him that nothing else had been damaged, so he poured himself a glass of white wine and sat at the table on the porch to assess the situation.

It had been a flying visit, that much was clear, and looked like the work of young vandals out for kicks. A flurry of destruction on the land, a run around the house, and the stone through the window to make the trip worthwhile was what it looked like to him. He wished there had been a note wrapped around the stone as it would at least give him something to go on, but there was nothing. Would a livid lawyer drive his luxury car up here to do this? Had Martínez flown into a rage because he had refused to work for him? Had Brian got drunk, lost his head, and come over to confront him about having deprived him of a few weeks' work? Had that stupid baker taken offence to his insinuation that he didn't dispose of a million euros and stormed over to kick a few lettuces around? None of these explanations seemed likely, but before ringing Vicente to ask his advice he racked his brains some more.

Néstor was the only one of his suspects who he thought capable of breaking the law, but from him he would have expected something either more subtle or more radical. He *might* have contracted some local yobs to come over on their bikes and do a little mischief, but there were no local yobs to speak of and he would hardly have made one of his rare visits to the village to seek out disaffected youths. Might he have explained his predicament to his Russian investors? Had the house been razed to the ground, maybe, but not this child's play.

After cleaning up the glass and taping some plastic sheeting to the window he decided to ring Pedro.

"Pedro, it's Jack."

"*Buenas tardes*, Jack."

"Did you see any cars going up the track to my house today?"

"Not that I remember, no, though I might have missed them if I was ploughing away from there."

"And no bikes or motorbikes?"

"No, what's happened?"

"Oh, there's been some minor damage done here. A broken window and some foolishness on the land. It looks like the work of teenagers, but I can't think who."

"Hmm, I'll watch out for anyone. Pedrito bought me one of those mobile telephones and insists that I carry it. I'll ask him to put your number in it and I'll call you if I see anyone going up or down the track. I'm away for barely an hour at lunchtime, unless it's raining."

"Thanks, Pedro, I appreciate that. I'll go to the village in my car from now on and can be back here in no time if you ring."

"I will be vigilant."

"One more thing, Pedro. I've been going through all the people who might have something against me and the one who stands out is our friend Néstor. He made me a generous offer on the house, you see, and I turned him down."

"He still pesters me, but I must admit that I don't discourage him completely. I'm having a surveyor in to divide the land and then my children can do what they like with it; except Pedrito, for now."

"It would be good if Pedrito's part were the closest to my land. Then we would still be neighbours," Jack said with fingers crossed.

"That's true. Yes, perhaps I'll arrange that, but don't worry too much. My other children are all very solvent and may not wish to sell. I for one will encourage them not to, but I suppose if the offer is very generous they might."

"Yes, I guess they might feel tempted to accept an offer that will not be repeated when people start to see sense." Jack tried to remember if Pedro was a churchgoer. "Still, it would be a pity if when you earn your eternal rest you have to look down on your land desecrated by houses and pools," he said with a chuckle.

"Ha, when we go, we go. I'll see nothing from my niche in the cemetery."

"No, I suppose not."

Jack took a sip of wine and rang Vicente. He didn't answer his house phone, so he tried his mobile.

"*Sí?*" Vicente bellowed over the sound of loud Latin music.

"Vicente, it's Jack here," he bellowed back.

"*Un momentito.*" The music subsided and a closing door cut it off completely. "I'm in Petrer, dancing."

"I guessed as much. I shan't disturb you now. What time will you be up in the morning?"

"Why? What's the matter?"

"Oh, a little damage has been done to my house and I wanted to ask your advice."

"I can be there in an hour."

"No, no, it's nothing. Little more than a broken window. I'll ring you tomorrow morning."

"I'll come round at nine. Don't ring the boys in green before I arrive."

"The *guardia civil*? Oh, I wasn't going to ring them."

"Well don't. This is *my* case and they will merely make the arrests."

"Ha, all right, Vicente. Come at ten and the *almuerzo* will be ready."

"Good, now I'll return to the arms of my teacher, Gabriela. We were working on my *Merengue* and I don't want her to transfer her attentions to another."

The following morning at half past nine Vicente's car rumbled up the track and Jack saw Salva in the passenger seat. Vicente sprang from the car and marched towards the porch with Salva following at a more leisurely pace.

"Show me," Vicente said.

"A good morning to you too." Jack stood up and led the two men over to the land. "This is what I think they did. I think they parked or left their bikes and came over here first. They pulled out the poles, kicked a few lettuces and broke those branches over there. Then they walked round the house and couldn't resist throwing a stone through the window." Jack led them round to the back of the house and pointed to the taped pane.

"You shouldn't have done that yet," Vicente snapped. "There may have been fingerprints."

"On the window? I've only touched the stone once, so there should still be some prints on it, unless they wore gloves."

"I doubt it," said Salva. "It looks like the work of kids, but why come out all this way?"

"We must look at motives," said Vicente. "The motive always comes first. Who are our suspects?"

Jack reeled them off and explained how he might have angered each of them.

"Néstor is *my* number one suspect," said Salva. "Not him personally, but to have sent some yobs to do it."

"But there aren't any yobs in the village, are they?" asked Jack.

"Why the village?" said Vicente. "He works in Alicante, remember. A hundred euros and a little map is all they would have required."

"But surely they'd have given better value for money after making the trip here? They didn't even touch the car," said Jack. "Anyway, let's have something to eat."

"Not just yet," said Vicente, before walking slowly away, inspecting the ground as he went.

Jack and Salva followed at a respectful distance as he made his way back to the vegetable patch. Salva giggled and nudged Jack, who put his finger to his lips.

"Damn it," said the sleuth. "We shouldn't all have walked round here. It's full of footprints, but there are more of these." He pointed to a large print.

"They're mine, I'm afraid. I walked round a couple of times last night too," said Jack.

Vicente shook his head and walked back to the gravel at the front of the house.

"Can you see signs of another car?" asked Salva.

Vicente ignored him and returned to the tomato plants. Hunched over, he approached the plum trees and continued past them towards the flimsy boundary fence. He stepped over the fence and began to cross an abandoned field of dead and dying almond trees.

"Should we follow Sherlock?" asked Salva.

"No, we'll spoil the trail. He's going down the other side of the hill now. I'll prepare the *bocadillos* while we wait."

"I'll get the wine out. He might go all the way to Alicante, or wherever the footprints lead him," said Salva, greatly amused by Vicente's antics.

When he finally returned the table was set. Jack poured him a glass of wine and waited.

"One person came here across the fields from an old track which begins at the road just outside the village," Vicente said, tapping a finger on the table as he spoke. "They wore medium-sized shoes, possibly trainers, and I think they reached the top of the track on a bicycle, though that is hard to say because the track is very stony."

"I know Pam went up there once to paint," said Jack.

"Pam?"

"The *inglesa* who owns the bar."

"I know her by sight. Ha, another suspect!"

"Hardly, Vicente. She's a great friend of mine. She's even helping me to find people to sell houses to."

"Hmm, did you ever spurn her?"

"Spurn her?"

"In love? Has she ever wanted anything more than mere friendship?"

"If she has she's always kept it well hidden. Forget about Pam."

Vicente sipped his red wine and looked at the table. "There's no use going to the *guardias*. They're too lazy to do anything about it, although I haven't met the new one yet. You'll have to report it if you want to claim for a new window on your insurance."

"Oh, that's too much hassle. I'll just have it replaced, once I see that there isn't going to be any more trouble."

"And when will you know that?" Vicente asked.

"Well, soon, I hope. Perhaps it was just a one off. I'll go about my business and shan't even mention it to anyone. Pedro Poveda's going to keep an eye on the main track and I'll come home for lunch every day next week. I'll have a look up that old track when I pass, if I have time."

"You could set hunting traps where those footprints are," said Salva with relish. "Cover them with leaves or something, and snap! Then we watch out for people with very bad limps."

"That's illegal, Salva," said Vicente, still in policeman mode.

Jack slapped the table and smiled. "Right, that's enough about that. Let's forget it and enjoy our *almuerzo*. Are you mastering the *Merengue*, Vicente?"

"Slowly. I wish to maximise my time with Gabriela. I'll need some more leaflets soon, by the way."

"Already?"

"Yes, I have asked my council colleagues not to remove them from the lampposts, but they are obliged to do so every few day. Most of the bars and shops in the town now have one displayed."

"Thanks, Vicente. I'll get some more printed soon."

"Give me some more too, and a few cards," said Salva. "We'll see which of us gets you a buyer first."

"Me, I'm sure," said Vicente, finally unwinding a little.

"It might be neither of you. Pam has spoken to an Irish couple who I'll ring later. They might like that old house we saw the other day, Salva."

"I still suspect this Pam woman," said Vicente.

"Oh, shut up and drink some more wine," said Jack, laughing and reaching for the bottle.

When his friends had left Jack washed up before taking a look at the footprints heading away from the plum trees. Sure enough there were two sets, one coming and one going, but they weren't very clear to him. Perhaps Vicente had done a course or something. He placed his size ten foot next to one and saw that they were somewhat smaller. Size six or seven, perhaps, but it was hard to say. If it would only rain again any future prints would be much clearer, but only fine weather was forecast for the coming week. He retraced his steps and poured himself another cup of coffee.

It might not happen again, but what if it did? He felt sure that next time the damage would be worse, but if he came home for lunch every day, made a few more quick trips back, and stayed in the rest of the time they might give up on the idea. If there *was* a next time he would have to go to the *guardias*, but what would he tell them? That it appeared to be a random act? The trouble with producing a list of suspects, or confronting them himself, was that he would mortally offend all but one of them. Something like that would get around the village and might end his years of tranquillity once and for all.

"I'm not going to spend the weekend worrying about it though, am I?" he said to Negro, who appeared untroubled by recent events. "Perhaps I should get a dog to keep you company, because you're not much use as a guard cat." He stroked him before going inside to fetch the Irish couple's number which Pam had given him.

He spoke to the man, Michael, who was indeed keen to see the house in the *aldea*, so Jack promised to arrange a viewing as soon as possible. He then called old Juan, who told him to drop by the *Hogar Pensionista* on Monday morning to collect the key, so he rang Michael back and suggested meeting at Pam's bar at twelve. He then called the number which Mario had given him and spoke to a man called Carlos. Carlos, who sounded quite young, said he had a partly finished chalet about five kilometres to the west of the village whose construction he'd had to abandon when he lost his job as a salesman for a company in Elda just after the crash of 2008.

"I'm working again now," he said, "but I can't see myself having the money to finish it for a long time. The roof's on and the bricks are rendered, but there are no windows, doors or floor tiles. It's on a ten thousand square metre plot of land which a friend keeps ploughed for me, but there's no boundary fence."

"Water and electricity?"

"Yes, and it's a legal build. I won't take less than eighty thousand for it."

"I'll try to get at least that then, more if possible. I just charge a thousand euros."

"That sounds all right. I'll explain where it is and you can go and take a look. You won't need a key to get in."

"No, I suppose not."

"And I'd rather sell to a foreigner if possible. I don't want anyone local finishing the house of my dreams, as I used to call it."

"I deal mostly with foreigners and I shan't mention it in the village."

"No, I'd prefer you didn't." Carlos gave him directions and Jack promised to do his best.

Whenever he had the phone in his hand he got an urge to call Encarna, but she would be celebrating her birthday with her children and he felt he was too recent an acquaintance to disturb her. A text message wouldn't be so intrusive, he thought, so after much fiddling with the phone he managed to wish her a happy birthday for today or tomorrow – she hadn't said which day it was – and promised to ring her on Monday.

Receiving a cheerful reply within five minutes took his mind off the vandalism and he strove to keep himself entertained for the rest of the weekend. He finished the amusing Graham Greene novel on Sunday morning and started reading the book about the American Indians. After reading the introduction he already felt a great deal of affinity with them. They had prospered for thousands of years without harming the flora or fauna of the continent, and then bang, along comes the white man and destroys their way of life within a couple of hundred years.

"Change and decay," he said to Negro as he fed him morsels of fish from his dinner plate. "Let's hope there's not much more of *that* here while we're still around."

19

Jack drove away from his home at ten to eight on Monday morning hoping that it would be as he had left it when he returned at lunchtime. Josemi was inside the old house when he arrived and he told him that he would be unable to lunch with them, this week at least, and explained why.

"That's bad," Josemi said, before placing the ladders he was holding where he planned to start work. He lit a cigarette and sat down on an old chair. After taking a long drag and exhaling he spoke. "The way I see it, from what you've told me about the people who want to buy your house, is that they could all be in it together, or at least three of them. Néstor, Martínez and the mysterious Russian all want the same thing, so they could have put their heads together and come up with the idea of harassing you until you say, to hell with it, I'll just sell. Les could be involved too, if they've kept the Russian business quiet and are using him as a standby option. What makes you think that Néstor's the only one who'd break the law? From what you've told me this Les might be a nasty piece of work too."

"Hmm, that's a good point. I just thought that being in a foreign country might hold Les back, but I guess it might have the opposite effect if he doesn't take the police here seriously."

"Not many people here take the police seriously when it comes to solving crimes. I think having three separate forces – locals, nationals and the *guardia* – makes them less effective. Are you going to confront the suspects?"

"No. I'm still hopeful that nothing else will happen, but if it does I'll call the *guardia civil*. If I challenge them all I'll make myself very unpopular."

"That's true. People here bear grudges for a long time. Sometimes they even become hereditary."

"All I want is a quiet life," Jack said, shaking his head. "I've a few errands to do this morning, so I won't be able to help you as much as I'd like."

"Don't worry. Amadeo and his men will arrive at nine to start installing the windows. I'll work around them as well as I can. You could take one of them to your house to measure for a new windowpane."

"Yes, I want to make at least one trip back this morning anyway."

Amadeo arrived in a large, brightly-painted van at ten to nine with two young workers who immediately set about unloading the windows. Jack asked him if one of them could spare twenty minutes to pop over to his house.

"They can't, no, as they'll be working nonstop until lunchtime, but I'll come once I've given them instructions. Have you chosen the doors yet?"

"Yes, I think so."

"Good, I'd like to be done here soon. I have to do a school in Calasparra next."

"A lot of windows."

"Yes," said Amadeo, before walking away to issue orders.

By the time Jack had mixed a bucket of *yeso* for Josemi, Amadeo was waiting in the doorway. As Jack drove out of the village he told Amadeo what had happened.

"And that old track just there is how they got to the house," he said.

"Scum," was Amadeo's only reply.

Jack unlocked the door and led Amadeo to the bedroom. The captain of industry made a note on a little pad and left the house.

"It's a standard size double-glazed unit," he said when Jack had caught him up. "I'll bring one tomorrow. Do you expect more trouble?"

"I don't know, but there could be."

"Then we'll replace the unit just before we leave." He stopped in the middle of the driveway and looked around. "Do you have a shotgun?"

"No."

"A pity. If it were me I'd stay at home until they returned and fill their legs with buckshot. More discipline is needed in this country. More discipline and a stronger work ethic."

"Yes, I guess so," said Jack, doubting that anyone who knew Amadeo would dare to break his windows or kick his lettuces. His own enemy, or enemies, clearly saw him as easy prey.

He dropped Amadeo at the house and drove to the *Hogar Pensionista* to pick up the key from Juan.

"Stay for a game of dominos and a glass of something," the old man said.

"Another time, Juan. I must dash."

"You youngsters don't know how to relax."

Jack returned to the house and set to mixing *yeso*. He was amazed at the speed at which Amadeo and his men worked. He and Josemi felt guilty when they left for their *almuerzo* and decided to make it a quick one.

"You're in a hurry today," said Pam.

"Yes, but I'll be back to meet the Irish couple in an hour." He decided not to tell her about the vandalism, but did ask one favour. "Pam, when Les next comes in to drink beer, or whatever, could you give me a quick call?"

"Yes, of course. Do you want to speak to him?"

"No... I'll explain some other time. Let's just say I want to know his movements."

"Very mysterious."

After mixing a couple of buckets of *yeso* for Josemi, Jack was back in the bar at twelve. Pam introduced him to Michael and Imelda, a friendly, fit-looking couple in their fifties, and Jack suggested they go to see the house right away. It would do his cause no harm to look busy, he thought as he drove out of the village onto the main road, and he knew there was a good chance that their faces would drop as a soon as they saw the decrepit house.

They greeted the old man who was sitting in the same spot as last time and Jack led them over to Juan's house, observing their reaction.

"It would be a... challenge," said Michael, glancing at Imelda.

"It's a money pit," she said. How much is the owner asking, Jack?"

"Just thirty thousand."

"Hmm, it's cheap and it would make a fine house, but... have you got anything else to show us?" she asked.

"No, not just now... no, wait, of course I have. A new property that I saw last week. Well, it was new a few years ago and needs finishing, but it comes with a lot of land."

"Are there any neighbours?" asked Michael.

"Not really. I think there's a *finca* about half a mile away where they live all year round, but that's about it. Would you like to see it?"

"Why not?" said Imelda.

Jack drove past the village on the main road and tried to remember where Carlos had said the house was. He had the directions on a pad in his pocket, but didn't want them to know that he hadn't even seen it. He turned off onto a lane and saw a new-looking bungalow in the distance. On approaching it he was relieved to see that it was windowless.

"This is it," he said as he rolled to a halt on the weed-ridden gravel outside the front door. "It's got connections for water and electricity and the paperwork is all in order. It just needs windows, doors and flooring."

"And paint, a fence, a proper patio and all the fixtures and things," said Imelda as she walked inside. "How much are they asking?"

Imelda's forthright manner made him reconsider his initial idea of asking for a round hundred thousand. "He's asking ninety, but I think he'd accept eighty-five."

"Eighty-five plus at least another twenty-five to finish it, as opposed to thirty plus... God knows how much to finish the other one," said Michael. "What do you think, dear?"

"Both are options, certainly better ones than the overpriced rubbish that Marta showed us, but I'm not really convinced."

"Well, we're in no hurry to decide," said Michael. "You'll be wanting to get back, Jack. I can see that we've interrupted your work this morning.

Jack looked down at his bare, dusty knees and scuffed work shoes. "Yes, I'm doing up a house that I bought in the village."

"Is that one for sale?" asked Imelda.

Jack dragged his mind away from the absurd thought that his house might be aflame as they spoke – he had even looked over in that direction for signs of smoke – and focussed on Imelda's question. He thought quickly.

"For sale? No, it's not for sale, but I might rent it out when it's finished. Some people who come over like to spend time in an area to see if it's right for them, you see, so somebody will probably rent it for a year or so."

"Can we see it?" Imelda asked.

"Of course, I'm heading that way now."

On the drive back Jack congratulated himself on his quick thinking – quick for him, anyway – and resolved not to appear too eager.

"It's certainly a hive of activity," said Michael as he got out of the car.

One of the front windows was being lifted into place as Amadeo appeared in the doorway wiping the dust from his hands. "Do they wish to see the house, Jack?"

"Yes."

"Pepe, Jacinto! Come out for a smoke while these people look at the house."

The two grateful workers left the house, followed by a bemused Josemi, trowel in hand.

"Take a look, though there's still a lot of work to be done," Jack said to the couple, before joining Josemi in the shade.

"Who are they?" Josemi asked him.

"A pleasant Irish couple who I just showed a couple of houses to. Then I had the brilliant idea of telling them that many people rent for the first year while they decide if they like a place."

"You're becoming a sharp operator, Jack." Josemi patted him on the shoulder. "I only hope that I'll be so effective when I start working for my cousin. I don't want to be just a driver for long."

"I'm sure you won't be. It's surprising how true the phrase *'la necesidad es la madre de la invención'* can turn out to be. Let's see what they say."

"I hope it's worth the bucket of *yeso* that will now be spoilt," said Josemi.

"*Es una casa muy bonita*," said Imelda as she walked out of the door, smiling.

"And they speak Spanish too," whispered Jack. "Or at least she does."

"Good, I wouldn't want complete heathens to buy the house," said Josemi.

"Rent rather than buy, I hope," Jack said before approaching the couple.

"I see you speak Spanish," he said to Imelda.

"We both do, but not very well. I suppose being in the village would help us to improve."

"I'm sure it would."

"How long will it take to finish the house, Jack?" asked Michael.

"Oh, not long at the rate we're going."

"And how much would the rent be?" asked Imelda.

"Oh, I don't know," said Jack, because he really didn't. "Something reasonable."

"We want to come out, with our furniture and everything, about two months from now. Will it be finished by then?" asked Michael.

"Definitely. I hope the smell of paint will have gone by then too."

"We'll think about it," said Imelda. "Thanks for showing us the houses and let us know if there are any more to see. We'll be around for a few days yet."

"I will. It's been a pleasure to meet you," said Jack, fighting off the impulse to give this assertive lady a little bow.

After pouring the spoilt *yeso* into a cardboard box in the skip, Jack mixed two more for Josemi before taking his leave and driving home for lunch.

When he passed through the gateposts and saw that his home appeared to be untouched he relaxed a little, but it was only after touring the house and inspecting the land that the fluttery feeling in his stomach subsided. For how many more days was he going to feel like this every time he came home? Perhaps he should take Amadeo's advice and stay put – minus the shotgun, of course – but had he done so today he wouldn't have met Imelda and Michael. No, he must keep himself busy and hope that some house buyers would appear so that he could continue to pay Josemi his wages without having to make another trip to the bank.

After a hasty lunch of tinned soup and defrosted bread he sat down in his easy chair to read for half an hour. He was shaking off his drowsiness and preparing to leave when the phone rang.

"Hola?"

"Hello, I'm ringing about a leaflet I've just picked up in Yecla," said a deep, male voice in what Jack thought was a Midlands accent.

"Yes, I'm Jack. Are you looking for a house to buy?"

"That's right, somewhere near here, if possible."

"Right, well I operate mainly a bit closer to the coast than Yecla, roughly between Monóvar and Jumilla. It's a little less cold in winter and a bit greener than there," he said, pleased at his spontaneous patter.

"What have you got to show me?"

"What kind of house are you looking for?"

"One in a nice village, ideally."

"Do you want something ready to move into, or are you looking for something to restore?"

"Oh, nothing too run down, and with at least three good bedrooms."

"Well, I might have just the thing for you here. It needs little more than repainting and I think the lady who owns it is just about to do that."

"Could I see it this afternoon? At about six?"

"No problem." Jack gave him directions to the village and more precise ones to Pam's bar.

"I'm Stewart, by the way."

"See you later, Stewart."

Jack thought it apt that the person who left the leaflet should also be the owner of the house that he aimed to sell. He was about to call Encarna but decided to leave it for half an hour to ensure that he didn't catch her when she was driving home from work. He drove back to the village and mixed a bucket of *yeso* before stepping outside to call her.

"Encarna?"

"Hola, Jack."

"Happy birthday for… yesterday?"

"Yes, it was. Thanks."

"I'm calling for two reasons; one business and one pleasure."

"Well let's get the business out of the way first."

"Somebody wants to see the house, at six. An *inglés* who picked up a leaflet in Yecla of all places."

"Ha, that's fate. Luckily I got my sons to move some of that old furniture out of the way, so you can see how the main rooms might look with a coat of paint. Pick up the key from here at a quarter to six if you like. Now, about the other reason for your call."

"Oh, I wanted to ask you if you'd like to have dinner one night this week."

"Sure. How about me cooking you dinner here on Thursday?"

"That would be great. Anyway, I'll see you in a couple of hours."

"Ciao, Jack."

By half past five Jack saw that Amadeo and his team had fitted most of the windows, so he made his final choice of doors, apologised once again to Josemi for being such a slack labourer, washed his hands and face, and headed to Encarna's.

"Here are the keys," she said, smiling around the half-closed door. "I'll be decently attired when you come back."

Jack met Stewart, a slim, bespectacled, rather sunburnt man of forty, and whisked him away from Pam's to see the house.

"What do you think?" Jack asked after leaving him to wander around the house alone.

"Like you said, it doesn't need much more than repainting, and perhaps new tiles in the bathroom."

"Is it just for you?"

"No, it's for me, my wife and our two kids. I'm out here doing a bit of research. They'll arrive at the weekend. We want to leave Derby for good and settle in Spain, somewhere where the kids can play out safely in the evenings."

"They'll be able to do that here. How old are they?"

"Five and seven."

"They'll pick up the language easily at that age and the local school is good. Do you and your wife speak Spanish?"

"We're studying. That's why we want to be in a village, so we can practise every day."

"And what... how will you make a living?" Jack asked.

"I work in IT and my wife edits books, so we can do that just as well from here, you see."

"That's all right then. Sometimes people come out thinking they'll find some kind of job easily, but they don't, especially not now, so they end up having to go back."

"No, we'll be fine – better off, in fact, as it's cheaper to live here – but thanks for asking." Stewart's smile reassured Jack that his rather prying and unprofessional questioning had not been in vain. A real estate agent wouldn't have dreamed of asking such things, but he had no intention of luring people here under false pretences.

"How much is it?" Stewart asked.

"Eighty-five thousand, which includes my thousand euro fee." That was twenty-five thousand more than Encarna had asked, but a paltry amount for two professional people.

"Hmm, it's not the cheapest I've seen, but I like it."

"Well, here's my card. Give me a call anytime if you want to see it again."

"I might well do that, Jack."

* * *

"Well, did they like it?" Encarna asked as she led him into her dining room.

"He did, yes. A nice *inglés* whose wife and two young children are coming out at the weekend. I think we'll hear from him again."

Encarna stepped into the kitchen and returned with two small glasses of beer. "I should get it painted, really, shouldn't I?"

"Well, it would look much better. Thanks for this." He took a long drink and put the glass down on the dining table.

"Do you want to do it, Jack?"

"No, it's a job for a proper painter who has all the equipment. Felipe's the best in the village. I could call him and ask him to give you a quote."

"You could do that, but what about this Brian fellow who you used to work for? Isn't he looking for work now?"

"Hmm, he's got a couple of spray guns, and his son to help him, but I think Felipe would do a better job."

"As you wish. Are you not going to sit down?"

"Not now, thanks. I feel scruffy and I have to get home to see about a few things. What time on Thursday?"

"About eight?"

"I look forward to it."

They kissed on both cheeks and Jack headed for his car. It was considerate of her to have remembered him mentioning that Brian was struggling to find work, but what he had said was true. It was a job for a painter and if he gave the work to Brian he would be denying Felipe a job that was rightfully his. Perhaps some building work would come up soon that he could pass on to Brian, but each man to his trade. As he drove off the road onto the track to his house he felt that nervous flutter in his stomach which only subsided after he had walked around the house. Today was Monday, so that made three days without incident.

"We'll be able to relax a bit soon," he said to Negro, who was sitting outside the front door waiting for his dinner. "But not just yet."

20

By *almuerzo* time on Tuesday Amadeo and his men were so far ahead of schedule that he relaxed his iron grip and allowed them to go to the bar for half an hour. Jack pointed them in the direction of Mario's, before inviting Amadeo to go along to Pam's with him and Josemi.

"I always breakfast well at home, but I will accompany you today," Amadeo said without taking his eyes off the cement he was smoothing.

"Pam, this is Amadeo, the faster window installer in the west."
"Hola, Amadeo. What can I get you?"
"Just a *cortado* for me, please."
The men sat down and Pam busied herself with their breakfast order. Since Jack and Josemi had been eating a mid-morning *bocadillo* every day, a few of her regular customers had begun to follow suit, which she much preferred to making them sad-looked toasties at lunchtime.

One or two locals had begun to drop in for coffee too, which pleased her even more.

"Pam is helping me to find buyers for the houses that I'm trying to sell," Jack said to Amadeo.

"Ah," he replied, stirring his coffee for the third time.

"That's one of the leaflets she made for me over there," Jack said, keen to get some conversation out of this enigmatic man who he might never see again after today.

Amadeo glanced at it, nodded, and sipped his coffee.

"So will you finish today?" said Jack, about to throw in the towel.

"Of course. We'll stop to fit your window on our way home." Amadeo stood up and walked over to inspect the leaflet more closely. "Your name isn't on it," he said on resuming his seat.

"No, but it's on my cards. Look, here's one." He pulled a card from his shirt pocket and handed it to him.

"On the card there is nothing but your name and number."

"Well, I don't like to advertise myself too much. The taxman, you know," said Jack, although he had already decided that if his house selling prospered he would try to make some contribution to the nation's coffers.

"But not just *Hacienda*, I think. It is also because you are a discrete man," said Amadeo, his lips curling upwards ever so slightly.

"That's true too," said Jack.

"Give me a couple of leaflets and a few cards. I occasionally see people who may be interested. I'll leave you to finish. I must go to collect my men from the other bar." He patted the table with his hands, stood up, and left.

"He likes you," said Josemi.

"What's he like with people he doesn't like?"

"Cold, icy cold. Don't forget the leaflets and cards. If he's asked for them it's for a reason."

"No, he's not one to waste energy. He seems more German than Spanish in his... discipline."

"There are more like him than you think. Spain would have a strong economy if it weren't for the stinking politicians. Let's get back."

Once Jack had waved off Amadeo and his men, he poured himself a glass of wine and sat down to enjoy the sunset. It had been a very good day. The windows and doors were in and his own window repaired. Mario had rung him about another house in the country and he had received a new enquiry, this time from a Dutchman who had peeled a leaflet from a Monóvar lamppost. He had printed more leaflets at Reme's and bought some fresh bread for the first time since his vexing phone conversation with Marco. The baker had not been unfriendly and was not a man capable of disguising malicious thoughts effectively. Jack thought he could cross him off his list of suspects.

Things seemed to be moving fast and once he was sure that the assault on his house had been a one-off he could look forward to a much brighter future than the one he had envisaged a few weeks earlier. Meeting Encarna had done much to increase his optimism and he had dinner with her on Thursday to look forward to. He no longer felt anxious about the status of their relationship. They were friends and if they were to become anything more he was sure that things would take their natural course. They weren't kids, after all, and he very much doubted that Encarna was the type who would want to 'shack up' with him. She seemed too independent for that.

* * *

Wednesday was another sunny day and Jack decided to cycle into the village. As he pedalled slowly up the road he looked forward to getting back to normality; just Josemi, him and endless buckets of *yeso*. Now they would plaster all the walls, before laying the floor tiles which he would order from Ramón's once Josemi had beaten him down to proper builders' prices. Josemi would be much better at haggling than he was. Perhaps he would lunch with them today, if it wasn't too short notice for Esperanza. As he rode up the street to the house Josemi's head came into view first, but what he saw next put all thoughts of normality out of his mind.

The lower half of the house façade had been sprayed haphazardly with blue paint. There were swirls, waves, a few straight lines, but no words. The perpetrator hadn't spared the new windows and front door, which was Josemi's main concern. He took Jack's bike from him, fearing he would hurl it to the ground, and spoke in an even voice.

"You must ring the *guardias* right away, Jack. I'll go to buy some solvent from Ramón's and start cleaning the door. The windows will be easy to clean, but the door concerns me."

Josemi's practical approach impressed Jack and enabled him to dispense with the usual lamentations. "Yes, and the wall doesn't matter, because we'll be painting that anyway. I stored the *guardias'* number on my phone in case something else happened."

He found the number, called it, and told the officer what had occurred.

"We'll be over sometime this morning," said a sleepy voice. "Don't touch anything until we get there."

"We'll have to clean the door or the paint might stain it. It's a brand new one."

"As you wish," he said, before hanging up.

"Should I ring Vicente, do you think?" Jack asked Josemi.

"Later. Let's see what the *picoletos* say first."

"All right. Do you think I should tell them who I suspect?"

"I don't know. There are so many suspects and so little evidence that I'm not sure they would take you seriously, although you could tell them about the damage to your house too. Perhaps their presence will dissuade whoever did it from doing further damage."

"Possibly," said Jack, sorely tempted to ask Josemi for a cigarette. He hadn't smoked for fifteen years, but if ever there was a time when he felt like a fag it was now. "What gets me is that whoever is doing these things doesn't give the slightest clue as to what they hope to achieve. Do they want me to sell my house, stop working on this one, stop trying to sell houses, or what?"

"Or all those things. It still looks like the work of youngsters to me. I'll go to get the solvent."

Jack entered the house and sat down on a dusty old chair. Perhaps he should ring Néstor, Les, Martínez, and even Brian. He could simply tell them what had happened and ask them if they knew who might have done it, making it sound as though he didn't suspect *them* in the least. If they became offended he could insist that he didn't believe for a minute that they had done it, perish the thought, but that they might be able to help him and the *guardias* with their enquiries. Later perhaps, but what should he do about the damaged paintwork? If he left it as it was it would create a stir in the village and might produce some information. Imelda and Michael wouldn't be impressed, though, if they came back to see the house. Move to a village full of vandals or even xenophobes? No thanks. He rang Josemi and asked him to pick up some white paint from Ramón's.

By the time Josemi had returned and begun to scrub the door with solvent, a green and white 4x4 rolled to a halt outside the house. Two sombre men in olive-coloured uniforms got out and sauntered towards Jack. The older of the two men, whose heavy moustache made him look almost like a caricature of the *guardias* of Franco's day, gave a stony-faced salute and walked off to examine the paintwork. His partner, an alert, clean-shaven man in his twenties, didn't salute at all, but his friendly smile more than made up for his lack of formality.

"What's happened here then?" he asked.

"Just what you see, nothing more," said Jack. "But this is the second time in five days that my property has been damaged." He described the assault on his window, lettuces and plum trees.

"It sounds like kids."

"Yes, I can just about imagine that here in the village, though nothing as bad as this has happened in the fifteen years since I've been here, but three kilometres away from here too?"

"Hmm, where are you from?"

"I'm English."

"Really, your *castellano* is excellent."

"Thanks. Would you like to take a look at my house in the country?"

The younger man glanced at his colleague, who stood smoking a small cigar and watching Josemi clean the door, and frowned. "I don't think that will be necessary now, if the damage was so slight and the window has already been replaced, but I'll make a note of it in my report. Do you have any enemies here?"

"A couple of people were annoyed that I wouldn't sell them my house, and I outbid somebody else on this house here, but nothing more than that."

"Hmm, it does give us motives. I'll make a note of the names of the possible suspects."

He took out his pad and Jack reeled off the names of Néstor, Les, Martínez and, more reluctantly, Brian, before explaining what each of them might hope to gain from their hypothetical actions.

"A lot of suspects," said the *guardia*, closing his pad and returning it to his pocket.

"Will you be speaking to them?" Jack said, a little worried by the prospect.

"Of course not. There is no evidence. If I were you I would tell people in the village that the *guardias* have been and that you have given them a list of suspects which they have forbidden you to divulge. Go to the bars now and the news will be in every home before nightfall. In my short experience I've found this to be a very effective deterrent."

"That's an excellent idea, thanks. I'll do that."

"If there are further… misdemeanours, call us immediately, but I doubt there will be." He gave Jack a half salute, half wave and called his colleague.

"Did he ask you anything?" Jack asked Josemi when they had gone.

"Him? No, the lazy bastard didn't open his mouth the whole time he was here. He doesn't even drive the damn jeep."

"Well the younger one was quite helpful." He told Josemi what he had told him to do.

"Yes, that might work. Martínez will certainly hear the news and will pass it on to Néstor, if they are involved. I don't know if the fat Englishman will find out, though, if *he* is involved. Look, the door is spotless. I'll clean the windows now."

Jack looked at his watch. "Did you get the paint?"

"Yes, and a couple of brushes. They're inside the house."

"Great, thanks. We can paint this afternoon. I'm going to visit Julio's and Mario's now to tell them the story. I'll meet you at Pam's in about an hour and I'll tell her too."

"All right, Jack. Remember to stress the mysterious list of suspects. They'll like that, especially Mario."

Mario's eyes bulged on hearing Jack's news and the *guardia's* instructions. "Of course you mustn't tell everybody about your list of suspects, but your closest collaborators, surely…"

"I'm afraid not, Mario. Strict instructions. You should see the house. It's *covered* in paint."

"Too far for me to walk, but I'm sure others will go to take a look. Any luck with the houses yet?"

"I think I'm getting close to making my first sale, and I haven't forgotten our arrangement."

"I hope there is no more damage, or you'll need the money for repairs."

"Just make sure everyone knows what I've told you." Jack finished his wine.

"You don't need to worry about that," Mario said, pushing away Jack's euro coin.

"I haven't seen you for a while," said Julio.

"No, I've been busy. Pour me a glass of white, please." The bar was busy so Jack told him the news right away.

"Very strange. Paint, you say?"

"Yes, a lot of it, and all over the windows and door."

"But you have your suspects?"

"Oh, yes, but as I said, I'm not allowed to mention them. The *guardia* need to do things their way. There's a keen young officer working on the case. He expects to have some results quite soon." Jack drained his glass and decided to leave before the two glasses of wine on an empty stomach made him get carried away.

"I shall watch people's reaction to the news," said Julio, polishing his glasses on a clean napkin. "Don't stay away so long again."

"I won't." Jack proffered a coin.

"It's on me."

As Jack walked to Pam's he reflected that if he had news like today's every day he need never carry his wallet again. He ordered his *bocadillo*, told Pam a less dramatic version of the news, and joined Josemi at their table.

"So," Pam said in Spanish when she brought the cured ham and tomato sandwich over, "the idea is to get the villagers intrigued by the whole business and dissuade whoever's done the damage from acting again?"

"That's right." He looked around the bar at the half dozen British customers. "My only concern is that a certain large Englishman will not hear about it, especially if he's not getting out much."

"Ah, don't worry. I'll take care of that. Denise comes in sometimes with friends, and I'm sure the news will get back to her anyway, especially if I drop a few hints."

"Not big hints, though, Pam. He might not have anything to do with it."

"No, just tiny *pistas*. The whole expat community will know about this within twenty-four hours."

"And Mario and Julio will take care of the locals. I only hope it works. I'm sick of worrying about if they'll do anything more serious, like burn my house down or something. Just when everything else had started to go so well, too."

"Do I see a little love light in those eyes of yours, Jack?" Pam grinned and scratched her nose.

"Can you see any?"

"Not really, but you were spotted with an attractive lady in the new restaurant the other night."

"Good heavens. How quiet my life used to be up to a month ago."

"Not anymore. Not for a while anyway. Eat your breakfast and go and paint that wall. Imelda and Michael were in earlier and your house is still top of their list."

While Josemi got on with the plastering, Jack began to paint the house wall slowly, torn between letting the villagers feast their eyes on it and not having it put the Irish couple off should they decide to wander past. Several locals passed in the next two hours and Jack told the story to all those who stopped to look. After a first coat some traces of the blue paint could still be seen, but he decided to take a break and ring Vicente.

"The bastards!" his friend said. "And I'm working all day today. I suppose I could come round in a patrol car."

"No, you'll get yourself into trouble."

"I could say there's a suspect from Monóvar."

"No, don't risk it. I think the young *guardia's* idea is a good one."

"Me too. Young, you say? He must be new. Did the other one look like Stalin on an off day?"

"Yes."

"That's Pérez. A lazy, incompetent reactionary."

"He did give me a nice salute."

"Yes, he likes that sort of thing. Listen, I have an idea, but I won't be back till the evening. Take a good look at the house when you come in tomorrow."

"What are you going to do?"

"You'll see."

Having become accustomed to making multiple phone calls, Jack decided to ring Salvador too. He told him his well-rehearsed story quickly.

"Yes, it's a good plan. As luck would have it, I have to speak to Martínez on behalf of a client. I shall weave the story into our conversation."

"Be careful not to accuse him, Salva."

"Don't worry, I'll employ the subtleties of my craft."

Jack gave the wall another coat of paint and spoke to a few more people. Some of them had come right across the village to see the now erased spectacle, so he described it to them in vivid detail. He ate with Josemi and Esperanza and in the afternoon they forged ahead with the plastering. He felt less nervous when he drove back to his house, but walked round it all the same.

"That should be that, Negro," he said to the cat over dinner. "Tomorrow you'll have to dine alone, I'm afraid, as I'll be at my friend Encarna's." He held out a bent index finger for him to rub his mouth against, first one side and then the other. "I hope you'll meet her one day. I think you'll like her."

21

When Jack arrived at the house the next morning he remembered Vicente's last words and scanned the façade. There, high up, next to a cluster of cables penetrating the wall, he saw a rather old-style CCTV camera, its wire appearing to enter the house. He laughed and pointed it out to Josemi who had just arrived on foot.

"When did you install that?"

"It's the work of Vicente."

"It looks real enough. Perhaps he has another one for your house."

"Hmm, I don't think I'll need it now, do you?"

"Probably not. We had three calls yesterday evening, all friends asking for clues about the mystery of the century. That's how dull this village is."

"The duller the better as far as I'm concerned. Come on, let's get on with a dull day's plastering."

"Yes, we should make a lot of headway today."

The two men entered the house and admired one of the bedrooms that Josemi had finished. With the new window and door and smooth plaster it looked like part of a brand new house.

"Shall I get Alfredo in to fit the new sockets and switches?" Jack asked.

"I could do it, but I guess you should spread the work around a little. Federico will be here on Monday to fit the water heater and plumb the bathroom. Before we know it, we'll be done," Josemi said.

"And you'll be off to start your new career."

"Yes. I'm trying to get my cousin to take me on the payroll, you know, and I've told him that I think I can be more than just a van driver."

"What does he say to that?"

"He's coming round to the idea. He says he can hear a new determination in my voice. I told him it was thanks to you."

"No, a catalyst perhaps, but you just needed waking up. Have you been tempted to play the *tragaperras*?"

"Not a single coin. What a mug's game it is."

At half past six Jack suggested knocking off a little early. "I'm going to Encarna's for dinner," he confessed.

"Really? You kept that quiet. She's a fine woman."

"Yes, she is. We're just friends."

"Hmm, inviting a man to dinner is a bold move in this village, you know?"

"I guess it is. You don't think... I mean, if we ever become...more than friends, that she'll want to move in with me, or have me move in with her, do you?"

"If you asked me that about any other single woman in the village I'd have to say that it would be a strong possibility, but Encarna's different. She's more independent and more... cultured than most people here."

"I'm too old for her, really."

"Too old? Nonsense. What's ten or eleven years? And you have the mind and body of a younger man."

Jack laughed. "I'll leave now while my morale is high. See you tomorrow, Josemi."

"Yes, enjoy yourself."

* * *

Shaved, showered and dressed in ironed clothes for once, Jack arrived at Encarna's house with two bottles of the finest wine that the small supermarket could provide.

"Hola, Jack. You shouldn't have brought anything," she said as she ushered him inside.

"It's the least I could do. I didn't buy you a birthday present, after all."

"Next year, perhaps, although it's not a birthday I'm looking forward to."

"Fifty? A fine age for anyone who's fit and healthy."

"I am that, thank God. There's a corkscrew on the table. The red wine if that's all right with you. I'll be back in a moment."

Jack watched her leave the room and was glad she hadn't dressed up for the occasion, though her blouse and slacks were as impeccable as ever. She returned with a plate of freshly cut cured ham and placed it among the other appetisers she had prepared.

"I've heard the news about the vandalism to your house, or houses. It's terrible."

"Yes, I didn't mention it before as I'd hoped it was a one-off, but the *guardia* suggested that I spread the rumour about a list of suspects. It's nonsense, really, as they're not going to investigate, but it might stop the culprit from doing anything else."

"I hope so," she said, plucking an olive from the dish.

"It's all supposed to be a big secret. It has to be, really, or I could offend innocent people, but I don't mind telling you who I think might have done it and why." Jack told her the full story to date and she listened in silence. "Who do you think it might be of those people, Encarna?"

"Well, I don't like to speculate, but it seems rather odd. Like you say, of someone like Néstor you'd expect something more subtle or more drastic, but he's not so stupid as to go wantonly damaging people's houses. He's doing well for himself and this silly housing idea will be one of many he's considering. Martínez likewise has too much to lose. As for this Les fellow, I don't know because I know nothing about him. If Brian has been a friend for such a long time I doubt he'd do anything like that. Whoever has done these things has taken a big risk, especially spraying all that paint on the house."

"That's true. Anyway," he said, clapping his hands softly. "Let's hope that the supposed vigilance of the *guardia civil* will put an end to it all."

"I think it will."

"On a brighter note, I had a call from the man who saw your house, just before I left home."

"Oh, what did he say?"

"That he wants to see it again on Sunday, with his wife and children."

"Hmm, sounds promising. I'll get our dinner."

Encarna returned with two plates of lamb chops and steaming vegetables.

"This looks good. About the house; he seemed keen, so I told him you were asking eighty-five thousand for it."

"That's a lot."

"Not really. There are cheaper houses around, but this is a nice, quiet village and that's what they're looking for."

"I'll settle for the sixty that I asked for."

"You'll settle for the eighty that he'll probably beat me down to," Jack said, waving his finger and smiling.

"Don't forget your commission."

"Ha, do you think I'd charge you for helping you out?"

"As you wish, but if I don't pay you, this will be the last dinner you have in this house," she said, imitating his admonishing gesture.

"I couldn't."

"You can and you will. Give it straight to Josemi in wages if you don't want it in your pocket."

"All right then, and I mustn't forget Mario's little slice."

Encarna imitated the bar owner's goggling eyes and they both laughed. After dinner she allowed Jack to stack the plates in the dishwasher while she chose a Bach CD and put it on. They sat on the sofa to drink their coffee.

"Nice music. Bach, isn't it?"

"Yes, one of his violin concertos. How's the work on the house going, apart from the free mural that someone painted," she asked.

"Oh, I've painted over that already. It's going very well. The new windows and doors are in and I *might* have found someone who wants to rent it."

"Who's that?"

"An Irish couple who Pam spoke to in the bar. Nice people who are making an effort to learn Spanish. I wouldn't mind them living there at all, until they find a house to buy. By the way, do you know how much people charge for renting a place like that?"

"Well, as it's going to be like new, with a new kitchen and bathroom, I'd say you could charge at least five hundred euros a month."

"So much? That would be... well, that would be a nice little pension, if I could keep it occupied," he said, before resolving to change the subject away from himself and money. "Do you have any plans for the weekend?"

"I've a lunch to go to on Sunday at my sister's in Sax, but nothing else. Why? Are you going to suggest something?" She turned towards him and pushed her hair over her ears.

"Oh, I thought we could go for a walk somewhere. The forecast is good and it would be good to have a change of scene, for me at least."

"Me too. One of my favourite walks starts in the valley on the other side of the mountain to the north of here. You drive towards Yecla and then turn right along a smaller road to a picnic area. That side of the mountain is much greener than the one we see from here and there's great view from the top."

"Shall we do that then? And get some lunch somewhere afterwards?"

"That sounds lovely. I'll try not to walk too fast for you, old man."

"Ha, please don't, though I'm still steady enough on my feet. What time shall I pick you up?"

"Around ten. That should give us plenty of time for the walk. Are you leaving already?"

"I'd better. I'm tired out after today," he said. His real reason was that he was beginning to feel rather amorous and feared that she would see it in his eyes. He wanted Encarna to be the one to decide if or when they were to become more than friends.

On the doorstep Jack's lips were heading towards her left cheek when she took his face in her hands and planted a light kiss on his lips.

"Sleep well," she said, "and I'll see you on Saturday."

When he cleaned his teeth an hour later he thought he could still feel that kiss on his lips. The first one, apart from his sister's, in how many years? Fourteen? It had been well worth the wait.

22

Jack felt like he was walking, or rather pedalling, on air as he cycled to the village the next morning. The sun was out, as it would be tomorrow for his walk with Encarna, and he looked forward to a good day's work punctuated by sociable meals at Pam's and Josemi and Esperanza's. He would be almost sorry when the house was finished and had already toyed with the idea of buying a real ruin to do up, but it wouldn't be the same without Josemi's company, skill and energy. No, he would do his best to rent the house, sell a few others, and return to his quiet life, a part of which he now hoped to begin sharing with Encarna.

He slowed his pace as the road steepened and told himself not to get his hopes up. Their relationship might come to nothing, or they might tire of each other after a while as had happened with him and Esme, but deep down he knew that he was unlikely to tire of Encarna. She had appeared out of the blue and he felt that this was his last shot at finding a companion. And if it didn't work out? Well, he had been content before and could be content again, but he rather hoped that theirs would be an everlasting... love? Was that too strong a word? Time would tell.

"The camera has kept the wicked ones away," Josemi said as Jack came to a halt.

"Yes, perhaps I ought to take it down in case the Irish couple come to take another look. I told them it was a crime free village."

"Oh, I'd leave it up for the weekend at least."

"Yes, it'll be a few days before we'll be sure that they've desisted."

"I'll finish my cigarette and we'll make a start. We can really make some progress today. How did you dinner with Encarna go, by the way?"

"Oh, it was very pleasant. We're going for a walk together tomorrow."

"Still just friends?" Josemi asked, flicking his cigarette butt away.

"Oh, yes."

"In that case, how about if me, Esperanza and the kids come along tomorrow too?"

"You're... more than welcome."

"Ha, I'm joking. You two need to get to know each other."

"Another weekend then? We mustn't lose touch once you start your new job."

"Definitely not."

"I'll start mixing."

On finishing the third bedroom they downed tools and adjourned to Pam's for their *almuerzo*.

"The graffiti on your house has been the main topic of conversation here since Wednesday," Pam said as she opened the wine and lemonade. "Half of them are worried that there might be anti-*guiri* feelings about and that their houses will be next."

"Anti-*guiri* feelings?" asked Jack.

"My words, not theirs. Nobody has any idea who did it though. They assume it must be the youth of village."

"I doubt it," said Josemi. "They know how to behave here, and there are too many pairs of eyes on them. Anyway, the paint must have been sprayed on in the middle of the night."

"Let's forget about it," said Jack. "Have you seen Imelda and Michael again, Pam?"

"Yesterday afternoon. They came in for a beer and were looking over some photos of houses. I think some estate agent had taken them for a drive."

"Right."

"*But*, they did say they were going to ring you," she said, smiling and raising her eyebrows.

"Well, fingers crossed they'll decide to rent first," said Jack, now set on the idea of extracting a small monthly income from the house.

On leaving Pam's they went to Ramón's to order floor tiles. Jack chose some large, rustic-style ones for the whole house and Josemi haggled mercilessly with Ramón.

"Shall we choose the bathroom tiles now too?" Josemi asked Jack once the deal had been struck.

"No, please don't. Go away and come back another day to choose them," said Ramón, shaking his head. "I'm still counting my losses."

"Liar," said Josemi. "We'll want the tiles delivering, of course."

"Oh, of course. If you like I'll lay them too," said Ramón, ushering them out of the shop.

After another session of plastering they allowed themselves an hour and a half for lunch in order to digest Esperanza's delicious seafood paella, before working steadily on until seven o'clock.

"Another good week's work," said Josemi, drying his brow on his t-shirt sleeve.

"Yes, apart from the little interruption midweek." Jack handed Josemi a small wad of notes which he pocketed without a word. "Have a good weekend and I'll see you on Monday."

"You too, and behave yourself."

Jack decided to push his bike up the last and steepest part of the track to his house. It was a lovely evening and he would enjoy it more on foot. He strolled to the house, leant the old bike against the wall of the porch, and called to Negro. Seeing him asleep on the porch, he made his usual tour of the house before climbing the three steps and taking his keys from his pocket. Another glance at the cat made him drop the keys to the floor. He was in a very odd position, his back arched strangely and his head twisted to one side. Jack leant down to stroke his neck and saw immediately that he was dead. After taking a deep breath and exhaling, he scanned the porch and saw something white in the far corner. He walked over and saw that there were three small pieces of fish, each coated in some kind of greenish powder, one half-eaten.

Rat poison, he thought. Rat poison ground down to a powder, but surely it doesn't work so fast? He returned to the dead cat and lifted his head. Blood, from a deep cut. Whoever had left the poisoned fish had waited around until he was weak enough to be caught and then finished him off, probably with a sharp rock. Jack walked down from the porch and over to the fruit trees. He headed towards his boundary fence and saw the footprints, deep and odd-looking. He realised that whoever had come across the abandoned field from the old track had walked back over the existing footprints. Very clever. Not so clever to hang around for hours until the cat collapsed though.

He returned to the house and unlocked the door. His first impulse was to ring someone, but who? And why? He was sick of involving everybody else in his problems. He took the brandy bottle from the cupboard and poured the last of it into a tumbler. He drank half of it before leaving the house by the back door with his spade. A dozen paces from the house he thrust the spade viciously into the loose, dry earth and within twenty minutes had dug a hole almost three feet deep. He went around the house to the porch, picked up the still-warm body, and carried it to the hole, where he knelt and placed it on the moister earth. He filled the hole slowly and by the time he had finished he had decided to ring the *guardia civil*.

"*Cuartel de la guardia civil*," said a woman's voice.

"Hola, I'd like to speak to the young officer, please."

"My husband's not in now. I can call Sergeant Pérez if you like."

"No, it's all right. When can I speak to your husband?"

"Tomorrow morning would be best, if it's not urgent."

"No, it's not urgent. I'll call tomorrow. Thanks."

Jack picked up the brandy glass and sat down in his easy chair. He would give the sunset a miss tonight and he knew that he wouldn't enjoy sitting on the porch for some time to come. The window, the paint, and now this; something much, much worse. And what next? Fire? An attack on himself? And all this was happening without so much as a hint from the perpetrator. Did they assume he would know who they were? Did Néstor, for instance, think that he would just pick up the phone and agree to accept the two hundred thousand? Did Les expect him to go round to his house to negotiate? Or were they all in it together as Josemi had suggested?

After ten minutes' thought he had planned what he was going to do. He decided to ring Encarna to tell her the walk was off.

"Hola, Encarna."

"Hola, Jack. Is something wrong?"

"Can you tell? Listen, someone has killed my cat. Poisoned it and whacked it with a rock or something."

"Oh, God."

"I've decided what I'm going to do. I'm not going to move from here until they come back. I'm going to leave my car down at Pedro Poveda's house now and I'm going to sit tight."

"Have you got a gun there?"

"No, and don't worry, I'm going to shoot them with something else, my camera. I'll speak to that helpful young *guardia* tomorrow morning and tell him what's happened and what my plan is. If he has no objections I'll stay inside until they come back and I'll get a photo, through the window if I sense any danger."

"It sounds like a good idea. Otherwise it could go on and on."

"Yes, so I'm afraid we'll have to put off our walk until another day."

"Don't worry about that. I'll come to see you tomorrow morning."

"You can't, I'm afraid. They might see your car, you see."

"I'll walk, up the old track you told me about."

"I'd rather you didn't, Encarna. You might bump into them."

"Good. In fact I'll bring my camera along too, and a pepper spray a work colleague once gave me. I laughed at the time."

"I don't think-"

"Don't think, just expect me at around ten tomorrow. I'll bring enough bread, milk and other stuff to last you a few days."

"Well, it *would* be nice to see you."

"Until tomorrow, then."

"Yes, until tomorrow."

Jack drove down to Pedro's and told him that he would explain later why he had to leave his car behind the outhouse. The old man didn't demur.

After walking slowly back up the hill he made a sandwich and opened a bottle of white wine. By the time he had finished it he was too tired to think anymore and took himself off to bed.

23

Jack was up at eight and headed for the door to greet the day, before turning right into the kitchen. Better get used to not going out, he thought as he switched the kettle on. While he waited for it to boil he lowered the plastic blinds on all the windows, leaving just an inch to spy through. After eating some toast he paced the rooms until ten past nine, when he rang the *guardia civil* barracks. He spoke to the young officer, who introduced himself as Amancio and agreed that his plan was a sound one.

"Just be careful, and ring me as soon as somebody appears. Make a note of my mobile phone number." He told Jack the number.

"Got it."

"Whether I'm on duty or not, I'll be there within less than half an hour. Just tell me exactly where your house is."

Jack told him and thanked him for going beyond the call of duty.

"It's nothing. I was in the Basque Country before I was posted here. Many people hate us there, so we were always vigilant. Here it's so boring that I'm glad to be of assistance."

"Thanks a lot, Amancio."

"I await your call, Jack."

Feeling somewhat uplifted by the young man's moral and practical support, he met Encarna with a cheerful smile when he answered the door to her gentle knock.

"Nobody saw me," she said, swinging a small rucksack from her shoulder and handing it to him. "There are a few provisions in there for you."

"Thanks. You look like a real hiker," he said on observing her stout boots and sporting attire.

"It's not far here, but I thought I'd better look like I was just out for a walk." She sat down and loosened her laces. "That poor cat."

"Yes, poor Negro. We'd only just become friends. I buried him behind the house."

"Poisoned, you say?"

"Poisoned and then beaten, yes. I feel awful about it. Would you like a cup of tea?"

"Tea? English style? I'd prefer coffee if you don't mind."

"I'll go and make it."

When Jack returned with two steaming cups, Encarna was deep in thought.

"What... how was the cat poisoned?"

"With some fish. The green powder on it looked like ground rat poison to me. I've buried the fish too, right over by the far fence."

"Do you keep any rat poison?"

"Me? No."

"Me neither. It's not something that most people keep nowadays. They get it when they need it."

Jack began to follow her train of thought. "Where can you buy it?"

"In the village? At Ramón's shop, I think."

"Do you think it's worth calling him?"

"Yes. The number's on here." She pressed some keys on her mobile phone and handed it to him.

"Ramón, it's Jack here."

"Don't tell me you want some more tiles already."

"Ha, no it's not that. Listen, do you recall anyone buying rat poison in the last few days?"

Encarna watched Jack's face as it expressed polite interest, growing curiosity, and finally consternation.

"Are you sure, Ramón? ... Yesterday, you say? ... And asking how much you'd need for a lot of rats? ... No, it's not important, really," he said, controlling his voice. "Thanks for your help. I'll be in for the wall tiles before you know it. See you."

He handed the phone back to Encarna and slumped into his armchair. She let him sit awhile, rubbing his temples with his fingers.

"What is it, Jack?" she asked when he lowered his hands and looked at her. "Do you know who did it?"

"I... I have a strong suspicion, but... I don't know... I need to speak to somebody to get to the bottom of this. I mustn't make false accusations on the basis of what might be just a coincidence." He gazed at her and she understood.

"I think you'll want to sort this thing out on your own. Am I right?"

"I think I'd better. I'm going to ask somebody round and I need to be alone with them. Can I come and see you this evening?"

"Of course, but you might still not want to leave here."

"I think it will all be over by then."

After walking Encarna to the edge of his land, he kissed her and offered her his hand to help her over the fence. She gave him a hug and told him to be careful.

"Tactful more than careful, I think," he said.

"Dinner will be ready at nine, but come sooner if you like."

"I will. Thanks, Encarna."

"Ciao, Jack."

He returned to the house, poured himself a small glass of wine, and picked up his phone. He dialled Brian's mobile number and waited.

"Hello?"

"Hi, Brian, it's Jack here."

"Hi, Jack. How's it going?"

Jack thought that his tone was like the one he used with customers. "I need to see you Brian, right away."

"What about?"

"I'll tell you when we meet."

"Are you coming into the village?"

"No, I think we'd better meet here."

"Well, this morning I've-"

"Come round now. I want you to come round now," Jack said before hanging up.

Jack looked in the fridge before taking a large bottle of beer from the cupboard and putting it in the freezer section. Ten minutes later he heard a van coming up the track and took the cold bottle from the fridge out to the table on the porch, along with a large glass and his own full wine glass. Brian jumped down from the van and strode towards the house. As Brian approached, Jack thought he looked more worried than inconvenienced.

"What is it, Jack?"

Jack held out his hand and Brian shook it. "Come and sit down and I'll tell you." He poured out the beer and pushed the glass over to Brian.

"A bit early for me," Brian said with a nervous laugh.

"Brian, has… has Liz been acting oddly lately?"

"Oddly? No more than usual, ha ha." Jack just watched Brian as he took a long drink of beer. "Well, to tell you the truth, yes, she's been acting strangely. First of all she threatened to go back to England, then she dropped that and… well, she practically stopped speaking to me." He drank some more beer and waited for Jack to speak. His shoulders were hunched and he appeared much smaller than the hulk of a man that he was.

"Has she been going out at unusual times, Brian?"

"Well, yes, and she's suddenly taken to walking everywhere. I ask her why and she just gives me that mysterious smile of hers."

Jack knew a few of Liz's smiles and could now picture the mysterious one. He took a sip of wine and decided it was time to take the decisive step.

"Have you heard about the trouble I've been having?"

"Oh, the paint on the house? Yes. Bloody kids, I suppose," he said, looking towards the fruit trees.

"As well as that I've had a window broken here and some more minor damage done. Whoever did it walked here across the fields from an old track over there." He pointed in the direction of the village.

"Right. You… you don't think that Liz has anything to do with it, do you?" Brian asked.

"Well, I'll tell you the last thing that's happened. When I got home yesterday I found that my cat had been killed."

"Killed?"

"Yes, poisoned, with rat poison, and then banged over the head with a rock. Whoever did it must have been here for a while."

"Yesterday," Brian said, and nothing more. He finished his beer.

Jack took his glass and went to the kitchen to refill it. He took the other bottle from the freezer and put it in the fridge. When he returned, Brian was gazing blankly over the valley. Jack filled his glass slowly to the brim and set it down in front of him.

"Thanks," he murmured.

"I rang Ramón and he told me that Liz had bought some rat poison on Thursday afternoon."

"And the paint," Brian said, almost inaudibly.

"Sorry?"

"I saw some blue stains on her fingers the morning after the house was vandalised. I didn't want to believe it. I told myself it could be ink. I wanted to challenge her, but I knew she'd go bloody berserk."

"It's a bad business," said Jack, nodding slowly.

"Why the bloody hell would she go and do things like that?" Brian was becoming angry now, but not with Jack.

"It's all to do with this stupid idea of Les and Néstor, isn't it? She must have thought that I'd get scared and sell up. Then they'd ask you to build a few dream houses and life would be wonderful, or something like that."

"I told her that project would never happen; not in so many words, but I made it clear. I also told her that Les was a bastard, but by that time his wife had put all sorts of ideas into that head of hers."

"She must have blamed me for buying that house too," Jack said.

"Yes, she hated you for it. It all fits together now. What can I say, Jack?"

"Now we have to decide what to do."

"I suppose you'll have to tell the police. I heard the civil guard had been round and were investigating." Brian took another drink of beer and let out a huge sigh. "I'm really sorry about all this, Jack."

"We have to look at this from Liz's point of view. I don't think she's a well woman and I'm going to make a suggestion."

"Go on."

"I think Liz ought to go back to England for a while. You once told me that her sister in Hexham was very supportive and I think she needs to go and stay with her. I also think she needs to get some help."

"You mean a psychiatrist or something?"

"Yes, psychotherapy I think they call it now, or maybe just plain counselling. She'll have to do that in her own language and I think she needs to get away from the… atmosphere here."

"I think you're right, dead right, but she'll never agree."

"Then you'll just have to tell her that if she's not on a plane home in the next few days I'll be going to the police."

"Would you do that, Jack?"

"It would be the very last resort, Brian, but it's the threat that counts, as long as you make her believe it. Look, she hates me now anyway, so why not make me out to be the baddie? Hopefully, in… I don't know… a year's time, me and her will be able to talk these things over."

"Maybe we'll all be back home by then."

"There's no need for that. Josh had been brought up here and-"

"And I've no bloody work to give him. It's been a hard slog for the last few years, as you know, always scratting about for the next job. Back home I can earn fifteen quid an hour as a brickie, no problem. I think Josh will have more future there too. Here he speaks the language all right, but he doesn't fit in as well as he should. He's a bit stuck between two worlds, if you see what I mean. Going back might be the best option for us."

"That's for you to decide. I would send Liz back first and have a good think about it. If you did decide to go back to give it a try there, I could try to rent your house out for you. That's what I plan to do with the one I'm doing up."

Brian smiled. "You're a good un', Jack."

"No better than I ought to be. Another beer?"

"Just one more, to give me courage for what I've got to tell Liz." Brian followed Jack's gaze to the corner of the porch. "Poor cat too."

"Collateral damage, I'm afraid. I was growing fond of it, but I'll probably be getting a dog soon anyway."

Jack took their glasses to the kitchen and refilled them. They sat in silent thought for a while before Brian spoke. "Liz will be out of here within a couple of days, but won't you have to tell the police something?"

"The one I've been dealing with is a nice lad. I'll tell him one story or another. He'll understand."

Brian drank half of his beer and stood up. "I'll be off now. If you don't hear from me it means that everything's gone to plan."

"OK, I'll give you a call in a week or so."

"And thanks for… understanding, Jack."

"Good luck, Brian."

* * *

"And that's the whole story," said Jack as they sat on the sofa after dinner.

"Poor woman, I hope she gets some help," said Encarna, stroking his hand.

"Me too. They can work wonders these days, and I think being back home will help."

"Wasn't the village her home?"

"Yes and no. Like Brian said about his son, people sometimes get trapped between two worlds. I imagine they'll all go back to England. Spain's not always the paradise that English people think it is, apart from the weather, of course."

"We'll have to go and visit your town sometime."

"Yes, we could pay a visit to sunny Accrington next summer perhaps. It's about time I saw my sister."

"Is she like you?"

"A bit younger and not so ugly. You'll like her."

"Ha, if she's anything like you, I'm sure I will."

"I'm a boring old thing, really."

"Not to me. More brandy?"

"Just a little. By the way, I got a call from Imelda this afternoon, the Irish lady I told you about."

"Ah, about them renting the house. What did she say?"

"She asked me if I could prepare a contract before they go back. We agreed on €500 a month, like you suggested. She thought it was cheap at the price. Josemi and I have until the first of November to finish the house.

"That's great news, Jack."

"It is, and it's all I really need to get by on, though I hope to sell a few houses too. One of those sales will pay for our trip to England."

"Ha, I'll be paying my way."

"Not for that trip, you won't. Anyway, it might well be your house that I sell first. The man who saw it wants to see it again tomorrow with his family." Jack stroked her hair. "Well, I'd better be getting home soon."

"As you wish." She put her hand on his cheek and turned his face towards her. They kissed – a long, loving kiss – and remained facing each other, hand in hand. "You can stay if you like, Jack."

"I will, soon, but not tonight. Maybe when we do… stay together, we ought to stay at mine."

"The village gossips, you mean? Ha, I'm far too independent to mind them, and it's not as if I make a habit of having strange men to stay. Never, in fact."

"Do you think I'm strange?" he asked, smiling.

"Strangely nice. I feel like I've known you for a long time."

"I feel that way too. It's funny we never met before."

"Yes, I don't think I'm any more sociable than you are really."

"The only thing better than being alone, for me at least, is being with someone you really… appreciate."

"I know exactly what you mean."

J.J.Birtwell,
Alicante, Spain
August 2015

Printed in Germany
by Amazon Distribution
GmbH, Leipzig